WOMEN IN PLATO'S POLITICAL THEORY

Women in Plato's Political Theory

Morag Buchan
Senior Lecturer in Political Theory
South Bank University
London

Routledge
New York

Published in 1999 by
ROUTLEDGE
29 West 35th Street
New York, NY 10001

ISBN 0–415–92183–X hardcover
ISBN 0–415–92184–8 paperback

Cataloging-in-Publication Data available from the Library of Congress

This book is printed on paper suitable for recycling and made from fully managed and sustained forest sources.

Printed in Great Britain

Contents

Acknowledgements

I wish first of all to thank Professor Elizabeth Vallance who was generous, kind and supportive in the early days of my research when everything looked absolutely overwhelming.

The Politics Division at South Bank University is a particularly friendly little 'family' and I thank every one of my colleagues for their encouragement, support and friendship. In particular I am grateful to Mike Hickox, Joe McCarney and Richard de Zoysa for the many good laughs which kept me going. Also to Dr. Kate Hudson for always being on hand to share a glass of wine and some much needed 'girl talk'. Much love and gratitude are also due to my 'room mate' at South Bank, Sam Hastings, for managing to boost flagging morale on so many occasions and for much more besides. I count myself extremely fortunate that Professor Jeffrey Weeks took over as our Head of School just as I was preparing my book draft and who took time in his busy schedule to read every word of the manuscript and give valuable advice.

My mother, now aged 90, and my father, 86, still think it is their job to look after me and I appreciate how well they have done so for so many years. Lastly, my son Al has been unfailing in his love and loyalty in the most trying times. The book is dedicated to him.

for Al

Introduction

When I decided, some years ago, to explore the role of women in Plato's political theory and confessed to friends that this was my project, I was usually greeted with two types of response. The first, given particularly pithy expression by a male colleague, ran along the lines of 'Oh, another of those "feminist perspectives" on something or other'. While this was said with a good-natured smile and was genuinely not meant to offend, it brought to my attention yet again the fact that enquiries of this sort still rested, for some academics at least, in that pastel pink area of 'soft options', philosophy shot through gauze. It did not aspire to the academic rigours of 'real philosophy'. I felt also that implicit in such remarks is a notion that such studies provide a cosy refuge for female academics who are cheating just a little in choosing a field which is, by its nature, not only intellectually less demanding, but in addition is especially easy for them, having as they do a biological head start.

In the early days of my research, therefore, I tended to fend off dubious witticisms with a firm insistence that it was no more intellectually impertinent of me to inquire into Plato's views on women than it was for any other academic to inquire into his theory of knowledge. I had not, at that stage, reached the point of arguing, as I was to do later, that the two are, in any case, positively linked, that the study of women in philosophy has implications for philosophy as a whole. It is not some isolated backwater, a relatively insignificant appendage to an otherwise respectable and respected academic discipline which could happily continue without superfluous fields of study being added to it.

I had only just begun to discover that a whole area of thought was opening out which challenged previously held views on philosophy, and which argued that philosophy itself might be seen to be 'gendered'; that the basic tenets of many philosophies, hitherto taken to be gender free, or gender neutral, were in fact presented in terms of the values traditionally associated with masculinity. Studying women in philosophy, therefore, was not relevant solely to women; its significance was much wider and far-reaching.

In the beginning, however, I merely stuck with my adamant assertion that the study of the role of women in any philosopher's

1

theory was as valid as the study of any other aspect of his work, and those who did choose to research into some other area never seemed to feel the need to justify themselves. I could study women in Plato simply because they were there.

Which brings me to the second most usual response to my chosen area of research, one which had to be taken even more seriously. This was an expression of genuine concern that I had bitten off more than I could chew, or more accurately, less than I could chew, in that Plato didn't say enough about women to justify a whole thesis, that women might be there but only just, and that an analysis of what he did say would fill, if not exactly the back of a postcard, certainly not more than a good-sized essay.

The basis of this concern was the mistaken notion that Plato's views on women, on female nature, on the role of women in politics and society, could be assessed solely, or at least largely, on what he says in Book V of *The Republic*. It is a notion which, once again, treats the study of women as a separate entity to be dealt with in isolation, divorced from the legitimate study of philosophy itself. And it was precisely this which needed to be called into question.

Book V of *The Republic* is, of course, where Plato outlines his social arrangements for women and children in the elite Guardian class of his proposed Ideal State, the state based on absolute justice. And what he has to say is radical to say the least, not simply for the period in history when it was written, when no notion of feminism, in any of the forms we understand it today, was on the political map, but for more modern times too.

It is a fairly radical form of contemporary feminism which suggests that women should be removed totally from the domestic sphere, and, in order to share the political arena with men, should not indulge in private marriages and should breed, by some controlled means, only as a matter of necessity for the continuance of the race.

In Plato's time this last was to be achieved by instituting periodic mating festivals where couples would mate with selected partners at the behest of the rulers. Nowadays modern technology and methods such as artificial insemination would further rid the reproductive process of the inconvenience of intimate relations, both emotional and physical, with the opposite sex. The principle, however, is the same.

Such a programme, mooted in the fifth century BC, was nothing short of startling and, it might be argued, not a little amusing into the bargain. So much so that some critics have tried to argue that anti-feminists, or more accurately, misogynists, of the period were also capable of a sense of humour and Plato was simply exploiting Socrates' pawky wit. Book V of *The Republic*, in other words, was not meant to be taken seriously. Alan Bloom has stated explicitly that Book V is 'preposterous' and Socrates expects to be ridiculed.

This is not an altogether unreasonable point of view when one considers that Plato's contemporary, the playwright Aristophanes, based two of his comedies, *The Lysistrata* and *The Assembly Women*, on the theme of women in public life. In both plays the women seize control of the city and in both utter chaos ensues. The idea of women maintaining social order were they to attain full legal and political status appears to have been too ludicrous to contemplate.

Yet most students of *The Republic*, while acknowledging that Plato never thought his proposals were a realistic, practical possibility, have come to the conclusion that he was making a serious point. *The Republic*, after all, is not a comedy. Though it is certainly injected with Socrates' witty asides, it is a serious work of moral philosophy. It seeks to construct the Ideal State, and it is Plato's contention that to attain this one must use all one's potential where it is best utilized in the interests of the state as a whole. Where women show potential, and he acknowledges that at least some of them do, that potential must likewise be utilized in the appropriate place. If this means that certain women will play a part in governing, so be it.

However, denying that Book V is a joke is one thing, assessing its full significance is another. I did have to concede at the start that this one book, in one dialogue, set in the context of Plato's entire philosophy, did not, at first sight, appear to amount to much research material.

Two things rescued me from this dilemma. The first was that however brief this passage might be, it was certainly not short of impact. It remains as controversial today as Plato himself acknowledged it was at the time.

The prelude to Plato's exposition on the role of women and children in the Guardian class, through the mouth of Socrates, is Socrates' contention that he has avoided the subject before because he foresaw all the trouble it would cause: his actual words are, 'You don't know what a hornet's nest you're stirring up'. This inclines one to believe that if it had not been of considerable importance Plato would have left the hornets alone. The treatment of women in the Guardian class could not, therefore, be dismissed as a mere tributary to the mainstream of Plato's political thought. It must be taken to be a crucial part of it.

This led me to my second life-line. This was the conclusion that Plato's views on women could not be isolated from his philosophy as a whole as his philosophy is, in itself, the foundation of his political theory. The one cannot be extricated from the other.

This meant that my research material, far from being miniscule, had taken on a new and quite daunting dimension. For although Plato only tackles the question of the able, competent woman directly in Book V of *The Republic*, his attitudes to female nature, women in general, and to one or two of them specifically, including Socrates' hapless wife, do appear elsewhere in the twenty-six authenticated dialogues. And they appear in a way which makes his proposals in Book V perplexing to say the least. At first sight Plato appears to be guilty of glaring inconsistency.

For disparaging or dismissive comments about the female sex in general are too numerous to recite. And this seems strangely incongruous with the notion that some women can be as competent as men, even to the extent of showing abilities which would enable them to enter the public realm and take part in the political life of the city.

It is certainly true that two of the women who make an indirect appearance in the dialogues, Aspasia in *The Menexenus* and Diotima in *The Symposium*, are depicted as women of some intellectual ability. But while each is exceptional, in her own way, neither seems particularly real.

Plato, of course, did use the names of real people, known to him, for his dramatic characters. Hence, for example, Plato's own brother, Glaucon, appears in *The Republic*; the playwright Aristophanes appears in *The Symposium*. But how much those characters and the opinions they expressed conformed to those whose names they bore is another matter.

The Aspasia of *The Menexenus* is an overbearing figure who allegedly makes Socrates recount one of her speeches. He claims to have been threatened with a flogging if he forgot. But is this the historical Aspasia, mistress of the famous Greek orator Pericles? The fact that in *The Menexenus* the dramatic Aspasia is said to have composed a funeral speech for the dead of the Corinthian war would seem to suggest not. The Corinthian war did not take place until after the death of the real Aspasia, as well as the death of Socrates.

Diotima, who is likewise depicted as instructing Socrates, this time on the meaning of love, is something of a mystery. We are told very little about her. She is described only as a 'woman' or sometimes 'priestess' of Mantinea. The existence of a historical character of that name has never been authenticated. Most scholars conclude that she did not, in fact, exist.

A further point of similarity between the two women struck me. Neither of them seemed to possess any particular degree of femininity or sexuality. What we are told of them is confined to their intellectual pronouncements and Socrates' assessment of these, an assessment which, though superficially deferential, is, in the case of Aspasia at least, sprinkled with irony.

However, the third woman who makes an indirect appearance in the dialogues, Xanthippe, the wife of Socrates, is altogether different from the other two. She appears to have no intellectual pretensions at all and is depicted solely as wife and mother, her role in childbearing made clear by the fact that she visits Socrates in his death cell with small child in tow.

She does not participate in the intellectual discussions which continue to take place between Socrates and his young friends and which comfort him in his last days. Instead, she disrupts the dignified calm of the condemned cell with hysterical weeping and wailing until she is banished by Socrates himself who admits that she is, quite simply, getting on his nerves.

In addition, he later chides those of the young men who begin to be overcome by emotion by reminding them that this was precisely why he had the women, Xanthippe among them, removed. Such is not rational, masculine behaviour. It is the behaviour of females.

A similar admonition appears in *The Republic* where Socrates asserts that men who show their emotions too freely are behaving in 'womanish fashion'. It is only one of many such comments which appear in the dialogues. Women are categorized alongside children, foreigners and slaves – those of inferior status in society. They are irrational creatures who do not have control of their emotions, that element of the soul which Plato believes to be the lowest part. Emotion is subordinate to spirit and ultimately to the highest element of the soul, reason.

Now it was clear to me at once that no serious academic argument could be based on three specific examples and general comments, however numerous the latter might be. It was unthinkable that I should try to argue that where women in the dialogues appear to be the product of Plato's creative imagination, they are intellectually competent, and that the more real the woman, the more intellectually barren she becomes.

Nevertheless, the distinctions drawn between these three women started to lead me in a definite direction. Just who were the exceptional women of the Guardian Class and where were they to come from? The only clue to their characters, or to the attributes they would have, did seem to lie in the description of two women who appear, on closer inspection, not to be much like women at all. They certainly did not conform to Plato's general and often stated view of female nature.

The argument that women of the Guardian class, robbed of their children who are removed from them at birth, divorced from their traditional sphere of influence, the home, are also thereby stripped of their very femaleness and turned into surrogate men, is not new. But if one accepts that this is, indeed, what happens to women in the Guardian class, then further questions need to be asked. If women of the ruling class are no longer real women, why does Plato bother to include them at all? Their role in childbearing cannot constitute the whole answer. An all-male class could still reproduce itself by means of mating festivals, simply choosing women from outside its own ranks to perform a biological function only.

Plato instead creates a ruling elite which includes Guardians who are, at least physically and biologically, ordinary females. What distinguishes them from other women and renders them extraordinary is that they are somehow intellectually different and that difference is one of superiority. They are intellectually superior to other women and, therefore, intellectually more like men. They have been specially selected for the Guardian class on the basis of Socrates' contention that where men and women have 'similar natures' they should not be debarred from performing similar tasks. Biological function in this connection is apparently of no account. Nature, it seems, is what determines one's ability, and where women have a similar nature to that of men, they may undertake tasks usually carried out by men.

Once again I was being led in a very definite direction towards very specific questions. Just what did constitute female nature for Plato? Or male nature for that matter? What was nature in itself? Was there such a thing as a gender free concept of nature?

This inevitably led back to the notion that it was the basic tenets of Plato's philosophy, not simply his explicit provisions for the governing of his Ideal State, which would hold most of the answers.

What Plato outlined for women in the Guardian class depended, certainly, on how he perceived the way in which justice would be served in practical, political terms. But this in turn depended on how he perceived justice in itself. And how justice was to be attained both in the state and in the individual depended, for both male and female alike, on the individual soul. Soul, at the heart of Plato's philosophy, held the key. And, as with the concept of nature, similar obvious questions arose.

What constituted soul in Plato's philosophy? Were there distinct male and female souls? Or was the concept of soul gender-free? It was this which led me into the gender debate.

The question of gender in philosophy has been a live and controversial one in recent years. This debate has involved the development and extension of questions previously asked by feminists about the ways in which women, female nature, women's reasoning powers, have appeared throughout philosophy. Women have, of course, frequently, been portrayed in less than favourable light, where they have been portrayed in any depth at all. Often they have simply been mentioned in passing. And where a male philosopher does mention them as an aside, it is frequently in disparaging terms, or at least in terms which appear at first sight to have no particular philosophical significance.

But more recent scholarship has started to focus less on the numerous misogynistic comments which appear in philosophy, or even on the direct and obvious implications these comments have for women's lives, and more on the ways in which philosophy itself may be seen to incorporate gender bias.

This type of enquiry clearly has implications not only for philosophy itself, but also for political theory. For if a political theory rests on a philosophy which has previously been taken to be gender free but can now be shown to be gendered, that theory itself can and must be challenged.

After all, a theory which rested on a philosophy which was genuinely gender free, or contained some notion of equality between the sexes, would be a significantly different theory. And the implications this would have for women's lives and political and legal status would be enormous.

I have chosen to analyse Plato in the above terms and I argue that Plato's philosophy is, indeed, a gendered philosophy, that it contains in its fundamental aspects, notions of gender and gender difference. That difference is the difference between the superior (male) and the inferior (female).

The foundation of Plato's philosophy is the concept of soul. It is Plato's belief that the soul of the human being, piloted by intellect, rises up in intellectual ascent to achieve true knowledge. It is my contention that an examination of the dialogues reveals that soul is a masculine concept. There is no distinct female soul. The female embodies only an inferior male soul and, since only the best souls attain knowledge, the implication this has for the female is obvious. The female is incapable of philosophy.

I argue also that Plato's views on women are not in the least peripheral, but central, to his political thought. *The Republic*, the Ideal State, rests on government by an intellectual elite, those with the highest capacity for rational thought, those who can restrain their emotions and physical appetites. Women, with inferior souls, are incapable of the highest form of rational thinking; they are thereby incapable of attaining real knowledge. Consequently, Plato's assertion that female Guardians will not only participate in the day to day running of the state, but will, in some cases, in the fullness of time, become the ultimate rulers, or Philosopher Kings, must be called into question.

Women display their inferiority of soul in female nature which Plato perceives to be passionate and uncontrolled as opposed to the restrained nature of the male. Those women who end up in the Guardian class do so because they can control, to a greater extent than most women, the worst aspects of female nature.

In the light of this I argue that political control in the Ideal State depends, to a large extent, upon control of female nature which stands not only in a relationship of inferiority but also of opposition to that of the male. It is thereby seen to be, potentially, politically subversive. The politics of the Ideal State and the creation of absolute justice therefore rest, not on the inclusion of able women in the Guardian class as a means of using all available talent, but on the contrary, precisely on the exclusion from that class of all things seen to be feminine.

Finally, I hope to show that a reappraisal of the role of women in Plato is relevant not only to an understanding of Plato's philosophy but to the ongoing debate on gender relationships within philosophy itself and the development of feminist perspectives within political theory.

The questions raised by Plato concerning women's relationship to men, to reproduction, to rational thought and politics, continue to be posed, and the problem of sexual identity in philosophy remains unsolved. Only by a reappraisal of philosophies such as Plato's, by asking different questions, or by asking the same questions in a different way, from a different perspective, is there the possibility of arriving at new and different answers.

In undertaking research into the work of a philosopher such as Plato, I have become humbly and acutely conscious of my own personal limitations. I approach the subject from the perspective of a political theorist first and foremost. I am not, by training, an historian or a classicist. I have certainly regretted more than once that I could not have had the intellectual pleasure of reading Plato in the original Greek.

But there are ever grey areas of overlap in academic fields, and where I have strayed into less familiar territory I hope that I have had some degree of success in my analysis and interpretations. I would like to think that students from more than one academic discipline would find something of interest in this book.

1 The Gender Debate

The question of gender in philosophy has long been a focus of interest for feminist academics of one hue or another. Over the past two decades in particular this 'gender debate' has generated a wealth of material on the subject of sexual identity in philosophy and has contributed much to feminist critiques of philosophical tradition.[1]

The origin of this type of research inevitably centred on the fact that women have frequently been portrayed by philosophers in ways which most modern feminists, notwithstanding differences and philosophical tensions within their various forms of feminism, would wish to dispute.

Dip into almost any period in history, the argument has gone, and look at what the philosophers of that period have had to say about women. It has usually been unflattering to say the least.

And indeed, even the most preliminary study of this kind produces sufficient evidence for saying that most philosophers did not rate women's intellectual pretensions very highly. What usually emerges from their writings, directly or indirectly, is at best dismissive of the female and at worst what Elizabeth Spelman has termed 'a veritable litany of contempt'.[2]

A few random examples serve to illustrate the point. Plato, writing in the fifth century BC, was prepared to allow a few select women into the elite Guardian class of his Ideal State, crediting them with some degree of intellectual ability and competence to govern. But he was not slow in other passages in the dialogues to pour scorn on their general lack of rationality and unrestrained emotionalism. More than once we find Socrates berating young men for emotional outbursts on the basis that this is the behaviour of women. And we are not left in any doubt that this is an inferior form of behaviour, springing from an inferior capacity to reason.[3]

While some have tried to argue that the very presence of women in the Guardian class indicates some early notion of feminism in Plato's philosophy, most feminist critics have seen this contention standing on very insecure ground. The female Guardians, after all, were exceptional, not typical women, and their number might have been intended to be very small indeed. Since Plato rejected the idea of individual marriage partners for his Guardians, a small group in any case, one may not even jump to the conclusion that the number of females would equal the number of males. At no point in any of the dialogues does Plato argue for a change in the position of women generally in Athenian society.

Aristotle, Plato's most famous pupil, is forthright and unequivocal in his assessment of the abilities of women. Women are, quite simply, the natural inferiors of men. Even their role in reproduction is diminished and rendered of secondary importance to the contribution of the male.

Aristotle states explicitly that menstrual blood is like male semen but in undeveloped form. The life force is male and is carried in the semen. Menstrual blood has to be acted upon by this life force, after which the female merely houses the embryo and nurtures it.

Aristotle is equally dismissive of the intellectual capacity of women. They do possess the capacity for reasoned thinking but once again it is in undeveloped form. So the female, for Aristotle, is both physically and intellectually inferior to the male.[4]

Where philosophers have been less direct in their views of female nature, they have often allowed their opinions to seep through the fabric of their 'more serious' arguments.

Thus Machiavelli, while not commenting explicitly on the female in *The Prince*, nevertheless, in advising the prudent ruler to use Fortune to his own ends, likens Fortune to a woman because Fortune is fickle. And being feminine and fickle, Fortune must be beaten into submission. What is more, such treatment is enjoyed. Fortune even prefers younger men who are more audacious with her.[5]

While some philosophers appear to accord women more status in society than do others, the nature of that status is frequently dependent upon women's relationship to men. We find, therefore, that Jean Jacques Rousseau, who speaks of freedom in *The Social Contract*, and of men attaining their freedom through the general will of the people, does not appear in any great hurry to extend this freedom to women.[6] For if one turns from *The Social Contract* to *Emile*, in which Rousseau outlines the appropriate education for a young man, Emile's female counterpart, Sophie, though she is likewise to be educated, is to be educated only in those things which will make her a pleasing partner for Emile.[7]

There was, of course, also a school of thought which adhered steadfastly to the notion that women were inferior to men because God said so. The argument that woman was created out of Adam's rib, thereby establishing that man came first, woman second, and that this would constitute the natural pecking order for all time, was one which Mary Wollstonecraft, writer of the first 'feminist manifesto', felt had gone too long unchallenged. And it needed to be questioned, she believed, before any practical change could occur in the social and legal status of women.[8]

This view was endorsed by more modern feminists who could point to many more such examples of women being depicted in an unfavourable light and who could expose, therefore, the obvious implications that these philosophies had for women's lives and social standing. Misogynistic comments were a glaringly obvious target for feminist attack and this was an unavoidable starting point for those who wanted to study women in philosophy. Jean Grimshaw has pointed out that documenting instances of misogyny in philosophy was not simply a relatively easy task but an essential preliminary in the study of gender in philosophy.[9]

In recent years, however, more important questions, germinating from this seed, have begun to be asked. It has begun to be questioned whether aspects of philosophy which are apparently unconnected with gender in fact contain notions of gender difference. Academic interest started to turn in the direction of questioning philosophy in general and the ways in which its basic tenets might be seen to be 'male' or 'masculine' in that they incorporated characteristics usually taken to be associated with masculinity.

This is a significantly different approach. For direct comments about women have often been taken to be passing observations which, while carrying serious implications for the treatment of women in society, did not impinge upon a philosopher's view of the nature of the world in general. It is precisely this which began to be challenged.

Spelman, writing in 1982, maintained that there had been a temptation to regard great philosophers' views on women as asystemic, as unofficial asides which were unrelated to the heart of their philosophical doctrines. She argued, to the contrary, that there are often conceptual connections between a philosopher's views about women and his expressed metaphysical, political and ethical views.[10]

What this means is that a philosophy cannot be seen to be masculine by virtue of expressed misogynistic prejudice alone. It must be analysed at a much more fundamental level.

In *Feminist Philosophers* Grimshaw argues in similar vein that questions about women still seemed very peripheral to mainstream philosophy and that misogynistic attitudes were often taken to be unfortunate relics of a past age. This view held that all that was necessary was to delete them from philosophy. Grimshaw maintained that this supposed that it was always possible to isolate what a philosopher said or implied about women from the rest of his philosophy, to cut it out and leave the rest intact. She questioned whether this could be done.[11]

But, of course, if, as Grimshaw suggests, it cannot be done and superficial misogyny, once removed from philosophy, leaves behind subtler and more significant prejudice, one must identify exactly how this prejudice reveals itself and how it affects the lives of women as it certainly must do.

Genevieve Lloyd argues in *The Man of Reason* that the very notion of reason is male, and that its maleness lies not in any superficial linguistic bias, but deep within western philosophical tradition.[12] But she maintains that this is actually a 'scandal to the pretensions of Reason', because, she points out, 'Gender, after all, is one of the things from which truly rational thought is supposed to prescind'. She adds that reason is taken to express the real nature of the mind in which there is no sex.[13]

This reinforces the point that it is necessary, in reappraising a philosopher's work in terms of gender bias, to look at aspects of it which do not necessarily express direct or indirect views on the female. One must examine those facets which are usually taken to be gender free in order to question whether there are areas of philosophy which are conventionally taken to be sex neutral but which are, in fact, imbued with notions of gender difference.

It is Lloyd's contention that the idea that reason is common to all human beings, transcending contingent historical circumstances which differentiate minds from one another, lies at the heart of our philosophical heritage. But she denies that in arguing the implicit maleness of reason one is adopting a sexual relativism, the notion that what is true or reasonable varies according to what sex we are. She argues, however, that in taking this position, one can see conceptual as well as practical reasons for the conflicts women experience between reason and femininity.[14]

Lloyd does not argue for a specifically female form of reasoning, and according to her argument reason might well be gender free, depending upon how it is defined, for in accordance with certain definitions, what constitutes reason might apply to either sex.

What Lloyd is saying, simply, is that if one examines the definition of reason in philosophy and finds that reason is consistently defined in terms of the exclusion of all things feminine, then it must be acknowledged, in the light of this, that reason is a male concept and not gender free.

In support of her argument Lloyd contends that one can go back to the beginnings of philosophical thought and discover that femaleness was associated with what reason supposedly left behind, the dark powers of earth goddesses, forces associated with mysterious female powers.[15]

This is an important point, for Lloyd is signalling here another aspect of the debate. This is the contention that reason is not only seen to exclude femininity, but femininity is seen to be threatening to reason. The two do not only stand as opposites, they stand in conflict.

Lloyd cites the early Greeks as an example of this. She argues that they saw women's capacity to conceive as connecting them with the fertility of nature. But rational knowledge had been construed as a transcending, transformation or control of natural forces. She adds, 'the feminine has been associated with what rational knowledge transcends, dominates or simply leaves behind.'[16]

Transcendence, dominance and exclusion are, of course, three different things. Lloyd does not pursue the distinctions between them, though in an analysis of any specific philosophy these distinctions might carry considerable significance.

Exclusion of the feminine from reason, for example, need not necessarily imply domination over it. Femininity need not be perceived as threatening to reason, simply as irrelevant to it. And while transcendence of femininity by reason implies the superiority of reason over something of a baser character, this need not imply that femininity is something to be feared. Femininity might be inferior, but not dangerous.

Alternatively, however, the three terms could coincide. They do not automatically exclude one another. Reason might be seen to transcend femininity which is not only in contrast to it but also inferior, and to dominate it because it is not only in contrast but in opposition, not only inferior but threatening. Different scholars have placed different emphasis on the various strands of the debate.

Carol MacMillan, for example, places the emphasis on the exclusion of femininity from reason, basing her argument on what she terms a 'spurious distinction' between reason and emotion. But she recognizes also the element of opposition contained within this distinction. MacMillan sees emotion and intuition as being seen to

be typically feminine characteristics standing in contrast to rational thought. She argues that this is a misconception of both reason
and intuition, and describes as fallacious the attempt to distinguish
between the private and public realm in terms of a strict contrast
between reason and emotion.[17]

Reason, or rationality, according to MacMillan, shows itself in
people's lives in many different ways. She claims that the supposi-
tion that analytical reasoning and the development of theory are
indispensable features of true knowledge does not demonstrate that
women have been inhibited from using their reason. Rather, she
maintains, this is a prejudice built on the notion that any activity,
whether it is scientific or not, must aim at general laws and rational principles.[18]

Women's intuitive ability according to this argument would not
be an innate faculty but one which was acquired through a kind of
training. It is MacMillan's belief that while many feminists have
recognized this, they have failed to see that since intuitive thinking
can be learned, that it is something for which there are rules for
proceeding, then it may appropriately be described as rational
behaviour.[19]

In other words, women's exclusion from a capacity for rational
thought might rest on a misconception of what constitutes rational
thought. And if intuitive thinking can be seen to be rational, then
women reason as well as men, though they may do so in a different way.

This is a seductive argument. If the focus of women's lives is
wholly different from that of men, then it is not unlikely that their
reasoning would operate differently. The contrast between men and
women, then, would not rest at the level of reasoned thinking as
such, but on the situation on which that thinking is brought to
bear. How men and women reason, in other words, would depend
on what they reason about, which aspects of their lives, or life in
general, they considered to be important, and what their objectives and priorities might be. The contrast, however, has not generally been defined in this way but rather at the level of what are
perceived to be typical male-female attributes.

MacMillan's contention that the distinction between reason and
emotion is a spurious one is likewise an extremely persuasive argument. It rests on an acknowledgement that emotion is, in itself, a
type of thought. This is often overlooked, or even disputed, and all
too often the description of emotions as 'feelings' has the effect of

relegating them to the level of the physical rather than the intellectual. But such feelings as love, anger, grief, while they may have attendant physical manifestations, are, nevertheless, part of a thought process, albeit a process that differs from the activity of pure reason. It might be argued, for example, that a female's protection of her offspring and the feelings this involves are not less rational because they are largely emotionally grounded. And notions of protection may involve less immediate and more subtle ideas of continuity and survival.

But such fundamental contrasts between male and female thinking continue to be drawn and their political significance is inescapable. Diana Coole extends the argument beyond the notions of contrast or exclusion to the idea of domination, that domination following inevitably from basic oppositions. Coole argues that western thought is fundamentally dualistic, that it involves a series of binary oppositions such as mind-body, subject-object, reason-passion.[20]

This is, indeed, the case. The notion of dualism in philosophy dates back at least as far as the sixth century BC when the Pythagoreans formulated a table of opposites on which male and female were featured. There were nine other contrasting terms: limited-unlimited, odd-even, one-many, right-left, rest-motion, straight-curved, light-dark, good-bad, square-oblong. These terms, however, did not stand in a solely descriptive relationship. Their significance, for the Pythagoreans, in terms of the nature of the world, was that they stood in relation to one another in terms of good or superior and bad or inferior. The terms mentioned first were associated with form, and this meant good. Those mentioned second were associated with formlessness, the inferior or bad.[21]

Such oppositions are the focus of Coole's argument, for she contends that such dualities spawn related antitheses in politics such as state-individual, public-private, universal-particular. The further, more significant polarity of male-female, she adds, often serves to give meaning to the rest.[22]

She identifies two consequences which ensue. The first is that the relationship of these oppositions is hierarchical. The first-named term, being superior, must dominate the second-named term. The second consequence is that the first-named term is posited as the standard or norm. It gains its identity by distinguishing itself from its antithesis, that which it is not. It is central, positive, while the opposite is negative, other.[23]

Coole is right to argue that political consequences clearly derive from this. If basic definitions are perceived in this way they stand as a justification for political arrangements which spring from them. They justify the male domination of the female in both private and public realms. Who could argue otherwise if it is accepted that the male is the superior, positive and central human being to which the female is by nature and by definition, the inferior?

Such symbolic associations Coole sees as having led a 'subterranean existence' in which they have structured western thought and its political traditions.[24] Her use of the term 'subterranean' is particularly significant in the context of the gender debate. This highlights yet again the fact that studies of women in philosophy need to dig deeper than the superficial instances of misogyny which abound, for hidden arguments for the subordination of femininity to masculinity might thereby very well remain intact after instances of overt misogyny had been challenged, even successfully challenged. Coole, in fact, points out that notions of the inferiority of the female are sometimes hidden in the fundamentals of theories which purport to speak of sexual equality.[25]

Identifying what she terms 'conservative' and 'radical' approaches in political thought, the conservative being that which sees natural differences between the sexes which are to be reflected in social place and function, the radical that which speaks of sexual equality, she argues that 'radical' is a misnomer. On closer inspection, she claims, this position has looked to identity rather than difference. The primary sexual opposition, therefore, is not overcome. What happens is that 'everyone is to be resolved into one side of the equation.'[26]

The result of this is not that the status of women is raised, but that emancipated women are those who can emulate the standards of masculinity. Therefore, Coole argues, the dilemma of sexual identity is not resolved; sexual difference is to be eradicated, but it is turned into an ideal of 'enlightened masculinity.'[27]

If one accepts this argument, rational thought is still male-defined and masculine, and the inclusion of women in this masculine world of reason does not in any way redefine, let alone elevate, the notion of femininity. Rather it posits the idea that inferior femininity need not necessarily be a static condition for some women, those who can rise above it and behave more like men. So both conservative and radical political theories contain serious implications for women's social and political standing.

In the first instance women may be legitimately debarred from political activity on the basis of their fundamental inferiority and the threat they present to rational male thought. In the second, where an attempt is made to include women in political activity, it often rests on the notion that female nature may be moulded or educated into emulating what is masculine, eliminating or at least subduing what is feminine. This in no way enhances the status or the idea of femininity within philosophy. It does not, as Coole has argued, resolve the dilemma of sexual identity. But it is this very dilemma which is at the heart of feminist thinking and which needs to be resolved.

GENDER AND FEMINISM

Feminists, however, have reached many different conclusions about sexual identity, and what constitutes 'feminist' thinking has itself been the subject of much debate and disagreement. As early as 1949 Simone de Beauvoir commented that enough ink had already been spilled quarrelling over feminism and perhaps no more should be said about it. But she added 'it is still talked about, however, for the voluminous nonsense uttered during the last century seems to have done little to illuminate the problem. After all is there a problem? And, if so, what is it?'[28]

Today, identifying the problem is still, in itself, a problem. There is a wide diversity of opinion among those calling themselves feminists and problems arise in using even the broadest of definitions. It would be inaccurate, for example, even to say that all feminists believe in the equality of all human beings, male and female alike, since some strands of feminism believe in the moral superiority of the female.

And it does not take the argument very much further to say that all feminists believe that women have been unfairly treated by men for centuries and this must change. The ways in which it needs to change and how such changes are to be wrought are still matters which are very heavily disputed.

Much of the disagreement surrounding male/female equality has naturally centred on the inescapable biological fact that it is women who produce babies. Indeed, the reproductive roles of the male and the female, and the possible connection this may have to their modes of reasoning, and consequently, their social role, remains in modern times something of a conceptual minefield. The very concepts of masculinity and femininity have often been seen to be determined in precisely these terms, a fact that some feminists would wish to change while others would not. One side of the argument has it that biological factors play no part in one's capacity to reason, the other that it is precisely women's role in reproduction and their relationship to children which gives them special insights and strengths, both intellectually and emotionally, which men do not possess.

Grimshaw cites this aspect of the debate as a major tension within feminism, pointing out that while some feminists wish to treat women as genderless persons, sexless bearers of human rights, others have wished to stress the importance of the female difference and to celebrate rather than deny this difference. Such feminists, she says, have argued that programmes which simply aim at equal rights for women or which adhere to the idea of a universal ideal of human nature fail to recognize the ways in which such ideals are usually male ones.[29]

In other words Grimshaw, like Coole, is arguing that to grant women equality in these terms is simply to allow them to enter a male-dominated world on male terms, and this does not allow that female difference, however defined, has any particular value or significance of its own. Equality in such terms is once again simply a matter of allowing women the opportunity to be equal to men if they can adopt male standards, male viewpoints and masculine behaviour. In short, if they can be more like men than women.

This can hardly be termed feminist, since it relies on the negation of all things feminine to the greatest possible extent. In fact it may be argued that this view is anti-feminist in that it perpetuates the assumption of male superiority. The male standard is that which women must strive to attain.

But if one rejects this notion, one must address the obvious questions which are implicit in that rejection. Is there an abstract, intellectual or spiritual level, beyond men and women's biological existence, on which they are the same? Or are women different in nature, other than in biological nature, from men? If so, in what ways are they different? What constitutes female nature? Do women have their own valid modes of reasoning?

The questions of the fundamental sameness or difference of men and women is explored by Prudence Allen in *The Concept of Woman*, where she argues that a limited number of alternative theories have emerged historically to explain the concept of woman in relation to the concept of man.

She identifies three main and two derivative theories. The main ones she terms: sex unity, the notion that men and women are not significantly different and that they are equal; sex polarity, the notion that men and women are significantly different and men are superior to women; and sex complementarity, the notion that men and women are significantly different but that they are equal.

The derivative theories she terms reverse sex polarity, which claims that women are superior to men, and sex neutrality, which, like sex unity, also argues for equality between men and women, but which differs from sex unity in that it ignores differences rather than arguing directly for equality of men and women.[30]

Allen's research, covering a period from 750 BC to AD 1250, and her interesting conceptual framework both highlight this central area of contention among modern feminists. The question is not simply whether men and women are basically the same or different. The real question is how do notions of sameness or difference affect the matter of equality between men and women?

The implications of sex polarity and reverse sex polarity as Allen has defined them are fairly obvious. One side claims dominance, or the right to dominate, by virtue of the essential inferiority of the other. It is the theories which she terms sex unity and sex complementarity which give rise to further problems.

What constitutes the unity in sex unity? Is it a genuinely androgynous position? Or does the matter simply resolve itself into a notion of one sex which, on closer analysis, emerges as the masculine? Is it, more accurately, the position that Coole has identified in her criticism of 'radical' political theory where she has maintained that everything is resolved into one side of an equation?

If, on the other hand, sex complementarity is pursued, and the notion of a fundamental difference, but equality, between men and women is accepted, the nature of the difference and the implications it carries for the lives of men and women needs to be explored. Allen herself acknowledges that there has been little interest in contemporary philosophical debate in establishing a secure foundation for a theory of sex complementarity.[31]

Sex unity theory, as she sees it, from the fifth century BC until the present day, devalues the materiality of the human person, the human body.[32] Her argument is that where men and women are seen to be the same, it is at a spiritual or intellectual and not a physical level. If Allen's interpretation of sex unity is accepted, if only the spiritual is seen to be of importance and the body plays no part in what men and women essentially are, the implications are obvious. The problems connected with reproductive difference, and the oppositions these have invoked, have been eliminated.

But this position is not acceptable to all feminists and notions of androgyny have been criticized, often on the basis that the so-called androgyny is simply the masculine by another name.

Among the feminist theorists who have been accused of positing a false notion of androgyny is Simone de Beauvoir. In *The Second Sex* de Beauvoir argues that if girls and boys were educated in the same way, surrounded by men and women who were undoubted equals, a child would perceive an androgynous and not a masculine world. She poses the question: 'Are there women really?'[33]

For her, the problem of femininity is rooted in women's biology. Woman, she says, is a prisoner of her biology. The ancients defined an absolute human type, the masculine. Woman, with ovaries and a uterus, was imprisoned within the limits of her own nature. Man, she says, thinks of his body as a direct and normal connection with the world, which he believes he apprehends objectively, whereas he regards the body of a woman as a hindrance, a prison. Woman is weighted down by everything that is peculiar to her body.[34]

The problem that this poses for feminism is that humanity is male and defines woman not in herself but relative to man. She is not regarded as an autonomous being. It is man who is Subject, Absolute. It is woman who is Other.[35]

De Beauvoir's point is that this is the result of false social construction placed upon women's biology which is taken as the determining factor in defining women's nature. In this sense woman is artifically created, hence the significance of de Beauvoir's question: 'Are there women really?' She is arguing that there are not, at least not in accordance with this definition. If women exist, their existence must be determined in some other fashion.

De Beauvoir argues that woman is determined not by her hormones but by the manner in which her body and relation to the world are modified by the actions of others than herself.

Woman, she says, is the victim of no mysterious fatality; the peculiarities that identify her specifically as a woman get their importance from the significance placed upon them.[36]

The problem will not be solved as long as femininity is perpetuated 'as such'. She argues that the abyss which separates adolescent boy and girl has been deliberately widened between them since earliest childhood. Things would be different if girls were to be brought up from the start with the same freedoms, demands, rewards and severities as boys, taking part in the same games and the same studies, surrounded by men and women who were undoubted equals.[37]

But this suggests that what de Beauvoir seeks for women is a place in the masculine world. The masculine is still seen as the human norm, the standard which women might attain were they not prevented from doing so. Girls must have their share of education, but in terms of de Beauvoir's argument, it is a very masculine type of education, that which has traditionally and very deliberately excluded the female. De Beauvoir wishes girls to be trained in the same situation, the same subjects and in the same way as boys. But this implies that she sees no possibility of gender bias, more specifically male bias, in this training. It is as if she sees the education of boys as somehow detached, or neutral where gender distinctions are concerned. There is simply learning, and males have been exposed to it while females have not. This is surely questionable. It is not unreasonable to ask whether, since girls have been excluded from this type of education, presumably on the basis of their lack of suitability, it is thereby education which upholds what are perceived to be masculine values.

In criticizing de Beauvoir on this point Grimshaw argues that in the matter of specific capacities or abilities, it is relevant to argue that women are as capable as men. However, where more general abilities or personality characteristics are concerned, one may ask why such things as sympathy or compassion should be regarded as of less value than abstract notions such as duty. She adds that one may also ask whether there is not something distorted or restrictive about conceptions of moral worth or autonomy which exclude characteristics seen as female.[38]

These are relevant questions, for while de Beauvoir speaks of androgyny, she also maintains there will aways be certain differences between man and woman. She argues that woman's eroticism, and therefore her sexual world, have a special nature. This means, she says, that woman's relations to her own body, to that of the male or to the child, will never be the same as a man's relation to his body, to that of the female or to the child.[39]

This seems strangely inconsistent. For de Beauvoir seems to be arguing here that the significance of a woman's biology is not restricted to its purely physical function. It does have some bearing on her relationships with others, and these relationships are distinct and different from those of men. But what exactly is the nature of woman's different relationship to others is left unexplored.

De Beauvoir's objection to the strictures of female biology appears to be that they spring from a male definition of that biology. She argues that woman must have her independent existence while she exists for man also. Each must recognize the other as subject, yet remain, for the other, an other.[40] She does not, however, attempt to outline how she perceives an 'independent existence' for women. Having argued that femininity 'as such' must not be perpetuated, de Beauvoir fails to offer a new definition of femininity. She does not say, in the end, what femininity is, she simply says what it is not. It is not as men have depicted it. Femininity from a feminist perspective is left unexplained. We are simply told that new relations of flesh and sentiment of which we have no conception will arise between men and women, and that they will be reciprocal.[41]

De Beauvoir also leaves largely unexplored the question of what will happen in this so-called androgynous world about the care and welfare of children. The comment that they will be surrounded by equal men and women at least implies the greater involvement of men in the matter of child-rearing, but this is not pursued. It is not an insignificant omission. For the care of children is another central issue in feminist discourse.

The argument that nature dictates that women have the babies, therefore nature thereby dictates that they rear them, and that their exclusion from other roles must be taken to be biologically determined, has, not surprisingly, been the subject of feminist attack. The second half of the argument, after all, does not in any way follow on logically from the first. That it is women and not men who carry the unborn child in their own bodies, labour and give birth, cannot be disputed. But the general care, nurturance and education of children is not biologically determined. It involves tasks which can be carried out by anybody, male or female, and not necessarily by the biological mother. It is not without satisfaction, perhaps even a degree of smugness, that feminists have pointed out that men, on occasion, when they set their hearts and minds to it, make very good 'mothers'.

Consequently, women's relegation to the domestic sphere on so-called 'natural' grounds has provoked arguments for some very radical solutions, including the one which states simply but effectively that it follows that if women stopped having babies, there would no longer be any justification for their exclusion from other roles.

This point was argued most forcefully by Shulamith Firestone. In *The Dialectic of Sex* Firestone argues that women, biologically distinguished from men, were culturally distinguished from human. Nature having produced the fundamental inequality in that one half of the human race must bear and rear the children for all of them, this situation, she argues, was later consolidated and institutionalized in the interests of men.[42]

Firestone does not explain how it is that nature dictates that women 'rear' the children, nor does she provide any argument to the effect that this is in any way inaccurate. She simply calls for the freeing of women from the tyranny of reproduction by every means possible and the diffusion of the child-rearing role to the society as a whole, men as well as women. She argues that childbearing can be taken over by technology and in light of this she calls for the destruction of the traditional family unit which, she says, breeds the psychology of power.[43] Her alternative is a 'household' rather than an extended family. The distinction is important, she says, because the word 'family' implies biological reproduction and some degree of division of labour by sex, and thus the traditional dependencies and resulting power relations.[44]

Freedom for women, sexual and political, in Firestone's terms, is attained at the cost of motherhood both in its physical and emotional sense. She acknowledges this sacrifice but questions whether it is, in fact, a real sacrifice. Pregnancy, she claims, is barbaric. Childbirth hurts and is not good for women. Artificial reproduction is not dehumanizing and development of this option should make possible an honest re-examination of the ancient value of motherhood.[45]

A similar denigration of the female's reproductive function, as well as a similar solution to the problems that motherhood poses for women, is offered by Jeffner Allen who argues that motherhood is annihilation of woman. Allen sees women as reproducing the existing world of men. Motherhood is dangerous to women because, she says, it continues the structure within which females must be women and mothers and, conversely, it denies females the creation of a subjectivity and an open, free world.[46]

Like Firestone, Allen believes the only way out of this dilemma is for women to give up their role in childbearing. She advocates a 'philosophy of evacuation', women's collective removal of themselves from all forms of motherhood, arguing that women are mothers because they have no choice. Without the institution of motherhood women would have that choice and they would choose to live differently.[47]

Allen denies that motherhood has anything to do with women's psychological or moral character. It has nothing to do with women's selflessness, sacrifice, nurturance or non-violence. It has instead to do with a history in which women have remained powerless by reproducing the world of men.[48]

However, similar criticisms to those levelled at de Beauvoir's notion of androgyny may be applied in both these cases. Both Firestone and Allen appear to see women's oppression as being their exclusion from another, superior world, a world filled with higher ideals and different values than those associated with motherhood. But this is the world inhabited by men, displaying masculine values and pursuing masculine goals.

For both these theorists freedom for women is the freedom to join this masculine world. And they can only achieve this by relinquishing a central part of female experience, which experience is not seen as having any value or relevance to female psychology. Male standards and male freedoms are those things from which women have simply been debarred because of their biological nature, and women must strive to achieve these freedoms by removing the obstacles to them, by abandoning their reproductive function. Freedom means being able to compete with men in a man's world and on equal terms.

Firestone and Allen analyse family solely in terms of power relationships and power in this context is the monopoly of men. Childbirth is seen only in terms of physical pain and its contribution to female subjection.

When Firestone questions the 'ancient value' of motherhood she is implying, like de Beauvoir, that this is an artificial social construction placed upon women's biology which continues to operate in the interests of men. She sees the removal of the physical side of child-bearing and the diffusion of the child-rearing role as freeing women from a situation which in itself has no value.

But once again it may be argued that Firestone is assessing 'value' in masculine terms. What has hitherto been seen to be the value of motherhood, in her view, has been merely an instrument of oppression, real value being in the masculine world of so-called 'freedom'.

Not all women, nor yet all feminists, would accept this view and could the 'ancient value' of motherhood be shown, in fact, to have a very special significance to the psychology of women, and could this significance be assessed in women's own terms, then the sacrifice which Firestone requires would not be such an empty one.

Firestone's often-quoted description of childbirth as 'shitting a pumpkin' is seen by many women as a crass over-simplification of the total experience of giving birth as only women themselves can experience it.[49]

This question of women's own experience is raised by Adrienne Rich in *Of Woman Born*. While accepting that motherhood can be restricting, isolating and oppressive, Rich argues that the experience of motherhood creates certain strengths in women.

But she draws the distinction between motherhood as experience and motherhood as institution. As institution, she says, it has withheld over one half of the human species from decisions affecting their lives. It exonerates men from fatherhood in any authentic sense, it creates a dangerous schism between 'private' and 'public' life, and calcifies human choices and potentialities. Women, she argues, become alienated from their own bodies by being incarcerated within them.[50]

But Rich does not conclude that women should, therefore, reject motherhood, at least not as experience. She argues rather that they should come to terms with their own physicality, step outside the limited male specifications of female biology. Such specifications, she says, have, in the past, caused creative or intellectual women to minimize links with the body, to insist upon being 'human beings'.

She argues that this reaction against body is coming into synthesis with new inquiries into the actual, as opposed to the 'culturally warped' power inherent in female biology. She calls for a 'healing' of the separation of mind and body.[51]

Rich, then, while acknowledging the strictures of female biology and arguing that these are culturally defined, rejects a solution which would deny mothers their maternal function and, in her view, prevents them from exploring the real nature of female biology.

This is a very different argument to that defined by Prudence Allen as sex unity and effectively argued for by Firestone and Jeffner Allen in their attack on all things maternal. Sex unity would seek to make women and men the same at a spiritual or an intellectual level and completely devalues the human body. According to this position equality can only be attained when the culturally constructed distinctions associated with biological function have been flattened out.

Arguments like that of Rich suggest rather that where women must compete with men on terms which involve the loss of a vital part of women's human experience, related to the peculiarities of female biology, this essentially constitutes a triumph of masculinity. It is the very essence and the value of femaleness which is lost or sacrificed in the process.

Coole has argued similarly that if attaining the same situation as men means that women are initiated into an identical world of man-made values and meanings, the victory might be a rather Pyrrhic one. Feminists, she says, need to consider whether human culture represents some neutral undertaking into which women might be assimilated without loss, or whether it exists as a particularly masculine project which, masquerading as a human norm, has suppressed an alternative feminine culture.[52]

Coole has raised an important question here, but a more important one inevitably arises out of it. What would constitute an alternative feminine culture? It is one thing to criticize sex unity theory both of past philosophers and of modern feminists who have adopted this position for failing to take account of the possibility of a typically female point of view, or of a redefinition of femininity in female terms, but a sex complementarity theorist would need to attempt just such a redefinition and identify typically feminine perspectives to have any credibility.

In accepting that this attempt has not yet been made, Prudence Allen comments that just as sex unity theory devalues the body, sex polarity places too much emphasis on the body in terms of male and female identity. Sex complementarity, she maintains, should avoid both extremes, and, while insisting on the importance of human materiality, must at the same time, present a comprehensive view of the nature of materiality. Only a theory which presents an integrated view of the place of materiality in human identity, she argues, can offer the possibility for fertile and creative relations between men and women.[53]

What is seen as sex complementarity here is a theory which would acknowledge women's biological difference from men, and accept that this difference has some bearing on female experience, relationships and modes of reasoning, without the total rejection of all things male.

According to this view the development of peculiarly 'feminist' perspectives in philosophy would depend to a great extent on exploring differences, contradictions and tensions, not only within philosophy itself, but within the various forms of feminist thinking.

It seems necessary first of all to identify the ways in which philosophy might be seen to be 'gendered' and to consider the implications this has had in the past, and continues to have for women's lives. It is also necessary, however, to consider whether philosophies which offer, or appear to offer, equality or equal opportunity to women in fact remain gendered in that they posit a male norm to which women must assimilate, often by the rejection of those characteristics which have been defined as typically feminine.

Finally, it is important to consider whether such definitions of femininity can be challenged and redefined. It must be questioned whether those feminine traits which are seen as having no value or relevance in the realm of rational thought, or as standing in opposition to it, might have value and validity of their own, might modify or complement, rather than threaten or destroy, all values seen to be masculine.

To attempt to locate Plato within the gender debate and to argue that his philosophy is a gendered philosophy appears at first sight to be relatively simple. He immediately fulfils the first and most obvious criterion. He makes frequent dismissive comments about the female in general, comments which indicate that he does not have a very high opinion of the intellectual abilities of most women.

However, his subsequent inclusion of certain women in the Guardian Class of his Ideal State has the effect of muddying the waters not a little. If he is serious about the abilities of these women then his view of gender does not polarize absolutely and finally into a notion of the rational male and the irrational female. Or at least it does not do so unless the inclusion of such women in the Ideal State serves some other purpose and his assessment of their capabilities is a smokescreen. But if it is, what is it that Plato is attempting to hide from us? And if he is not serious, if he is joking, as some have suggested, why is he joking? What is the significance of the joke in terms of gender and sexual identity? In short, if Plato is, indeed, located within the gender debate, just where is he located?

PLATO, GENDER AND FEMINISM

In any attempt to analyse the role of women, and consequently, the role of gender in Plato's philosophy, an obvious starting point is Book V of *The Republic*. It is here, after all, that we find his most direct comments on female ability, albeit limited to relatively few females.

However, it is precisely the exclusiveness of this assessment of certain women, and the stark contrast it creates between Guardian women and the female in general, which determines that the analytical net needs to be spread much wider.

Spelman, for example, comments that Plato's description of women's nature and his prescriptions for their proper societal niche have come under the scrutiny of feminists who wish to reject his views. She adds, however, that feminists, in their own theorizing, have continued to accept uncritically other aspects of the tradition that informs philosophers' ideas about women's nature.[54] In any analysis of Plato, she maintains, it is important to see the conceptual connections between what Plato says about women and other aspects of his philosophical positions.[55]

The failure of some critics to make such connections is without doubt the source of much of the controversy that has surrounded Book V of *The Republic* for some years. Interpretations have ranged from one extreme to the other. It has been argued, on the one hand, that Plato was a misogynist, typical of the society in which he lived, and, on the other, that he was an early feminist.[56]

Such differing views are hardly surprising. Plato's general belief in the inferiority of the female, appearing as it does in more than one dialogue, and juxtaposed with a political arrangement for the Ideal State which includes women in the ruling class, and at least implies that some will become the ultimate rulers or Philosopher Kings, is the source of this confusion.

There has been an abundance of explanations, designed to resolve what appears to be an inexplicable inconsistency, one which few critics felt inclined to attribute to a philosopher of Plato's stature.

There may even have been a degree of embarrassment on the part of some at trying to reconcile this apparent contradiction in Plato's position. As Susan Mendus has commented, 'When women read philosophy they tend to fall into an embarrassed habit of thinking that they ought not to criticize the ludicrous views which result, that it is unfair and anachronistic to think that people of this calibre ought to be able to avoid going into print with this sort of stuff'.[57]

It is possibly an attitude of this sort which has led some critics to give more credence to what Plato says about female Guardians than to his more general asides about women, and while not exactly ignoring the 'less acceptable' remarks he makes, to consider them somehow excusable in light of his 'real' views as expressed in *The Republic*. There are those, Wendy Brown and Arlene Saxonhouse among them, who have argued that there are distinctly feminine perspectives in at least some of Plato's philosophy.[58]

But Plato does appear to offer two very different views of the female, and it is inconceivable that he could have failed to notice that they were incompatible. One cannot, therefore, dismiss or overlook one set of opinions in favour of the other without having sufficiently good reason for doing so. And no good reason immediately springs to mind in a comparative analysis of the dialogues.

One obvious answer to the problem would be to argue that Plato at some stage simply changed his mind about women. But the trouble with this solution is that in the first place one can find no obvious or logical reason why he should have done so. In the second place, the dating of the Platonic dialogues does not support such a conclusion.

The dialogues, individually, cannot be dated with any precision. But historical research based on Plato's life, the odd reference in one dialogue to another which clearly, therefore, must predate it, and examination of literary style, have enabled Plato scholars to divide the dialogues broadly into three groups, early, middle and late.[59]

The Republic, with its revolutionary proposals for women Guardians, belongs to the middle period. But so also does *The Symposium* in which Plato depicts the spiritual ascent to real love as an exclusively masculine pursuit, taking time along the way to relegate the physical love of man for woman to the status of inferior animal behaviour.[60] *The Phaedo*, in which Socrates berates his weeping companions in his death cell for behaving like women, is likewise of this period.

That Plato was unwittingly contradicting himself from dialogue to dialogue, even in dialogues which were written in the same period of his life, seems unlikely, if not unthinkable. What is more, *The Timaeus*, in which Plato argues that souls are separated into the superior and inferior, and that the inferiors are placed in the body of a woman, is of the late period.[61] The argument, then, that Plato changed his mind about women and that *The Republic* represents his true and final thoughts on the subject is instantly vulnerable.

The dating of the dialogues would rather suggest that if Plato changed his mind at all then, from a feminist's points of view, he changed it the wrong way round, from believing in female equality to believing in female inferiority.

But Plato did not change his mind, nor is there any inconsistency in the dialogues concerning female nature. Plato's philosophy is a gendered philosophy and this position is not, and cannot be, argued from an examination of any one of the dialogues nor even on a comparative analysis of what he says from one dialogue to the next.

It requires an analysis of the fundamentals of Plato's philosophy as a whole to arrive at this conclusion. It is necessary to look at such basic aspects as Plato's theory of Forms and his theory of Knowledge to understand the role that women play.

For Plato, the attainment of real Knowledge, Truth, Love or Goodness depends on an intellectual ascent to an abstract realm of rational thought. But while intellect is the vehicle by which the ascent is made, it is the human soul which rises up. It is soul which holds the key to the significance of gender in Plato's philosophy. It is soul, therefore, which must be examined first.

2 The Masculine Soul

The concept of soul is one of the most prominent and significant in Plato's philosophy. The question of the soul's immortality is a recurring theme in the dialogues and one upon which Plato's theory of Knowledge rests. For Plato, Knowledge is arrived at by means of an ascent from a dark cave of ignorance and into the sunlight of Truth.[1] It is, however, by way of the soul, guided by intellect that this ascent is achieved and human reason arrives at the spiritual realm of the Forms, a realm of absolute, unchanging entities such as Goodness, Truth and Love.[2]

Plato also tells us that knowledge is the recollection of what individual souls have perceived before birth, travelling in the train of the Gods.[3] The nature of the soul, therefore, linked as it is to the attainment of knowledge, and to the perception of Goodness, Truth, Love and ultimately, Reality, is central to any analysis of the dialogues.

But what exactly constitutes the nature of the soul is not easily determined. The term itself may be taken to have more than one meaning, and there are problems in translation. The Greek word 'psyche' can also be used for 'life' or 'mind'.[4] And the Greek word normally translated as 'soul', according to G.M.A. Grube, more accurately means the 'principle of life' in any being. Whatever is alive must possess it, and the word 'psyche' was not, in very early times, automatically linked with the conception of immortality. Where a belief in immortality does appear as, for example, in Homer, and the part of a man which survived death was called the psyche, life after death was depicted as a shadowy counterpart of full-blooded life on earth. This meant that immortality, or life after death, did not represent a higher form of existence which it would come to mean in later thought.[5]

Grube's analysis traces the notion of the soul as the highest part of man to the Orphics, mystical teachers and prophets whose doctrines came from the East. The Orphics taught that immortality was no longer a pale reflection of earthly life but a release from the body which was seen as a tomb or a prison. Man aimed at the purification of his soul which, after many incarnations, would rise to perfection and be reabsorbed in the divine.

The process of purification as a way of life was developed by the Pythagoreans in the 6th century BC. They took the immortal psyche to be the intellectual power of man and the purification process took the form of strict scientific training. Grube contends that it was from the Pythagoreans that Plato took his notion of intellect as the noblest and the immortal part of man.[6]

He adds the caution, however, that once again translation causes problems. The words 'intellect' and 'intelligence' could not be taken to mean the denial of emotion. For Socrates and Plato the soul culminated in the intellect as its highest function. Consequently, 'mind' is a more suitable translation. The soul was that which directed or should direct men's lives, ruling over the body and its passions.[7]

Mind and soul, then, can be taken to be virtually synonymous in Plato's thought, but the nature of mind or soul is still unclear. It is not constituted of pure thought or reason, and while intellect is its highest function, there is also an element of emotion contained within it. Mind or soul, then, is not merely an empty vehicle through which intellect expresses itself. Intelligence and soul are clearly inseparable. Nevertheless, they are distinct, and soul, consequently, must have its own nature.

Plato is explicit about this in *The Timaeus*. For while he comments that intelligence is impossible without soul, the two are clearly not one and the same. The Creator, he tells us, wished to make all things good and, so far as possible, nothing imperfect. The world thereby came into being possessed of both soul and intelligence:

> When he considered, therefore, that in all the realm of visible nature, taking each thing as a whole, nothing without intelligence is to be found that is superior to anything with it, and that intelligence is impossible without soul, in fashioning the universe he implanted reason in soul and soul in body and so ensured that his work was highest and best.[8]

Perfection, then, may be seen to be a perfect combination of intelligence and soul. Body, created last, is of least account.

It is important to note, however, not only that soul and reason are distinct but also that it is soul which exists first. Soul predates all else, and in arguing for the immortality of the soul in *The Phaedrus*, Plato emphasizes this. He comments that it is necessary to form a true notion of the nature of the soul, and argues that all soul is immortal. This is because what is always in motion is immortal, but that which owes its motion to something else may cease to be in motion and therefore cease to live. Only that which moves itself never ceases to be in motion since it could not do so without being false to its nature. It is, therefore, the source and prime origin of movement in all other things that move.

Plato does not actually tell us how it is determined that the soul is always in motion, nor how it is that it is the source of movement in all other things. He simply asserts:

> Now a prime origin cannot come into being; all that comes into being must derive its existence from a prime origin, but the prime origin itself from nothing; for if a prime origin were derived from anything, it would no longer be a prime origin.[9]

Now this is a somewhat unsatisfactory argument and, as so often in the dialogues, it goes uncontested by any of the respondents. The nature of soul is presented here rather as being self-evident than the subject of any kind of logic or proof. But, proof or not, it is clear from this that Plato believes that everything which exists derives its existence from soul.

This is further emphasized as he expands on his notion of the soul's immortality. He argues that what moves itself, and is therefore immortal, may be identified with the 'essence' and 'definition' of soul. This is because all body which has its source of motion outside itself is soulless, but a body which moves itself from within is endowed with soul, since self-motion is the nature of soul. Once again, this is not subject to any proof, but Plato clearly thinks it is an acceptable argument and concludes:

> ... if then it is established that what moves itself is identical with soul, it inevitably follows that soul is uncreated and immortal.[10]

Nothing, of course, has actually been 'established'. But what we do have is Plato's adamant assertion that the soul is immortal and it is the soul from which all else springs. Intellect, implanted in soul, is not in itself a prime origin. Like everything else created it derives its existence from the prime origin. There is no thought without soul.

It is an assertion which is repeated in *The Laws* where Plato tells us that soul has been born long before physical things. He also indicates that it predates all other non-material things, though it has a close relationship with them. He argues that anything closely related to soul will necessarily have been created before material things. Opinion, diligence, reason, art and law, he tells us, will be prior to roughness, smoothness, heaviness and lightness.[11] Nature, and natural things, will be secondary products deriving from art and reason.[12]

While it is clear that the main distinction Plato wishes to draw is that between the physical and the non-physical, this also indicates that while abstract things may have a close affinity with soul, soul remains the prime origin from which everything else derives. Soul come first and, with its own identity, is not to be confused with intellect or thought.[13]

This distinction between soul as prime origin and derivative intelligence closely related to it is of particular significance when one comes to assess Plato's political programme for the Ideal State, based as this is on varying levels of ability in human beings. For if intellect is distinct from soul, it is clearly not intellect alone which distinguishes one human being from another, though this is what a superficial reading of *The Republic* might seem to suggest.

A further area of distinction clearly exists at the level of the self-moving prime origin through which intellect expresses itself but which is quite distinct from intelligence. And while it may be that similar intellects reside in similar souls, intellect obviously does not wholly dictate the essential characteristics of the human being. Intellect stands in relationship to other aspects of human nature. This proves to be vitally important in assessing Plato's view of the female.

For he tells us in *The Republic* that spirit and appetite are also both present in soul and the capacity of reason to control these two determines the soul's nature.[14] A soul, in other words, might be possessed of a high degree of intelligence, and yet be governed by its appetitive elements. Such a soul would be inferior to that in which a similar level of intelligence subordinates appetite and utilizes spirit.

Plato allows that men and women with 'similar natural capacities' should perform the same tasks in the Ideal State, and this has been interpreted as indicating his belief in the essential sameness of the male and female soul.[15] But 'similar natural capacities' in this context refers to practical or intellectual expertise. For example, he describes men and women with similar medical ability as having the same nature.[16] It is also worth noting that Plato is inconsistent throughout the dialogues in his use of the word 'nature', and one must frequently decide from the context exactly what he means.

At this point in *The Republic* he asserts that natural capacities are similarly distributed in the male and female sex and there is therefore no reason why women should not take part in all occupations with men, although he is not slow to point out that women will always be the weaker partners.[17] Nevertheless, he contends that there is no administrative task which is peculiar to woman as woman or man as man.[18]

But Plato's belief in these so-called natural similarities does not preclude a distinction between men and women at the level of soul. The 'nature' of men and women, defined in terms of intelligence or ability, does not constitute what Grube has termed the 'principle of life'. And in addition to his comment that women will always be the weaker partners, Plato also states that in general men are far better than women at everything.[19] So even at the level of ability a general distinction is drawn between the sexes, a distinction which relegates women to second place.

And while intellect alone does not constitute the essential soul, one cannot overlook the fact that the two are linked; indeed, they cannot be separated. Intellect has been implanted in soul by the Creator and resides alongside other human characteristics. Plato elaborates on this in *The Republic* in his explanation of the tripartite soul. In positing the Ideal State, founded on Justice, Plato also considers justice in the individual. Justice in the individual, as in the state, is achieved when all the constituent elements within it perform their proper function and harmony is thereby attained. The three elements of soul – reason, spirit and appetite – are in harmony when the highest element, reason, rules. Spirit ought to obey and support it. Such concord may be effected by a combination of physical and intellectual training, and once these two elements are educated to perform their proper function, they are placed in charge of appetite, which is naturally insatiable:

> They must prevent it taking its fill of the so-called physical pleasures, for otherwise it will get too large and strong to mind its own business and will try to subject and control the other elements which it has no right to do, and so wreck the life of all of them[20]

The struggle for harmony is very much an internal struggle, and Plato likens it to a civil war between the elements. When one rebels and gets out of control the elements of the mind are confused and displaced. This, Plato tells us, constitutes injustice, indiscipline, cowardice, ignorance and wickedness of all kinds.[21]

What Plato is saying here is that just as there are superior and inferior intellects, so also there are superior and inferior souls. The inferior are those whose constituent elements are in a state of disharmony.

Now Plato's contention that women, in general, are less able than men does not of itself indicate the inferiority of the souls of women. After all, whatever the level of reason in any soul, it stands in relation to spirit and appetite. As long as reason is in control of these two, the one harnessed to its support, the other subdued and subordinated, the soul is in harmony.

However, the frequent disparaging remarks which Plato makes about the personality of women in general, regardless of any intellect or ability they may possess, at the very least carries the implication that they have less harmonious souls. For what prompts such remarks is how Plato perceives female behaviour, not female competence. It is a question of how women conduct themselves, not how well they perform certain tasks.

When Plato discusses the education of young Guardian men, he stipulates that where they take part in dramatic representation they must not play the part of women. Women are depicted in drama as abusing their husbands, quarrelling with heaven, boasting of good fortune, lamenting in misfortune. They are also depicted in sickness, in love and in childbirth.[22]

Young men must not be permitted to take part in such representations because such is not the behaviour of rational human beings whose intellects are in control of their appetitive elements. Women are presented here rather as uncontrolled hysterics associated not only with the irrational but, inescapably, with the physical.

They are also associated with the uncontrollably emotional. In speaking of the effects of dramatic poetry Plato comments that even the best of us can be carried away by our feelings but in private grief men pride themselves on not behaving in this fashion: '... and we regard the behaviour we admired on the stage as womanish'.[23]

The emotions of women, then, are less controllable than those of men, although men may be vulnerable in certain circumstances. It is for this reason they are prohibited from depicting women in drama. They must be protected at all costs from an assault on their manliness. They must not, therefore, embrace female behaviour, even if they are only play-acting.

For Plato, education plays a crucial part in controlling the worst elements of soul, and this applies to women as well as men. However, much concerning the soul is already determined by pre-existence.

In *The Phaedrus* Plato tells us that soul traverses the universe appearing at different times in different forms. When it is perfect it is winged and moves on high governing all creation. It enters body only when it has shed its wings and fallen to earth.[24]

It is while travelling on high, in the train of the gods, upon the back of the universe that souls perceive the region of reality, apprehensible only by intellect, the pilot of the soul.[25] But some souls attain more of the vision of reality than others, and when a soul misses the vision it sinks beneath the burden of forgetfulness and wrong-doing and falls to earth. Souls are then born into human beings in varying degrees of goodness dependent upon the extent of their perception of reality.

The struggle to attain true knowledge again is the struggle to recollect what has been perceived in the journey with the gods. This is an easier task for some than for others. For while Plato acknowledges that every human soul has beheld true being in some degree otherwise it would not have fallen into the creature called man, not every soul finds it easy to use its present experience as a means of recollection:

> Some had but a brief glimpse of the truth in their former existence; others have been so unfortunate as to be corrupted by evil associations since they fell to earth, with the result that they have forgotten what they once saw.[26]

This means that before birth the better souls, those with the best perception of reality, while not guaranteed to achieve knowledge again if they have been corrupted by earthly existence, nevertheless begin with the advantage of having more of the vision of reality to recollect. Correspondingly, those who have seen less of the vision begin earthly life with a handicap. The success of the earthly, inner struggle to attain knowledge determines what happens to each individual soul. There will be future earthly incarnations, and ultimately a soul may find itself in the body of a beast as a result of wrongdoing in its earthly existence.[27]

Plato makes no distinction in *The Phaedrus* between the souls of the male and female but has indicated quite clearly that there is a distinction between individual souls in terms of superior and inferior. The male-female distinction, however, is drawn elsewhere. In the myth of Er at the end of *The Republic* Plato speaks of souls after death. We are told that each soul must choose its own future incarnation. The 'choice', however, turns out to be a matter of choosing from lots cast among them, after which they are shown the pattern of their future lives. The soul, in other words, does not directly choose a life; the lot is merely a number, interpreted into a life after it has been chosen.

The implication is that those who have led a good earthly existence in their previous lives will automatically make the best choice. The souls are told by Lachesis, the maiden daughter of Necessity, that Excellence knows no master; a man shall have more or less of her according to the value he sets on her. The fault, then, where one chooses an inferior future incarnation, does not lie with God but with the soul that makes the choice.[28]

But it has already been explained that the choice is by lottery; it is a blind choice. This would seem to indicate that there is an inherent goodness or badness which directs the soul which chooses. This, in turn, would seem to suggest that Excellence is part of the prime origin or, as in the case of intellect, contained within it and appears in varying degrees in individual souls.

Only when the process of the lottery has been fully explained does Plato add in the manner of an afterthought: 'And there was a similar choice of lives for women.'[29]

Now this instantly draws a distinction between the lives of women and the lives of men. If this were not the case both sexes would be able to choose from the same lots. But they do not; they choose from 'similar' ones. The fact that women face the lottery at all clearly means that women also face future lives of varying degrees of goodness, but if the lots must be different, then the lives must be different in some fundamental way. This raises the obvious question as to whether excellence in a woman is the same as in a man or, at least, if it appears in greater or lesser degree.

We cannot answer this question with sole reference to the Myth of Er. Only the distinction is clear, not the nature of it. But earlier in *The Republic* Plato speaks of his Guardian men and women as having 'gold' in their souls. It is this which fits them to rule.[30] Once again, a superficial reading of this would seem to indicate Plato's belief in the essential sameness of men and women, as does his allotting similar tasks to similar people, regardless of sex. But the later mention of excellence in the soul in the Myth of Er invites a retrospective reappraisal.

Just as excellence might be a different sort of excellence for a woman, as the separate lotteries would suggest, gold might be found in greater or lesser amount or in greater or lesser degree between the male and female. There is, after all, hardwearing 9ct gold and then there is gold of the utmost 24ct purity. Plato's contention that men are generally far better at everything than women appears to lead to an obvious answer concerning the female soul. It is essentially different from that of the male.

The distinction between the superior male souls and the inferior female souls is, however, no more than implicit in *The Republic*. It is quite explicit in *The Timaeus*. It is in *The Timaeus* that Plato describes the birth of the universe and of the soul and it is here that the superiority of masculinity is made clear.

THE SOUL AND MASCULINITY: THE TIMAEUS

The primacy of soul is repeated in *The Timaeus* where Plato tells us that God created soul before body, gave it precedence both in time and value, and made it the dominating and controlling partner.[31]

It is here that we also learn more about the nature of the soul and its constituent elements. The creator, says Plato, has mixed together three kinds of Existence: the indivisible, the eternally unchanging; the divisible, changing Existence of the physical world; and a third kind of Existence intermediate between the two. The same procedure has been followed with the Same and Different. An intermediate compound has been arrived at between their indivisible element and their physical and divisible element. All compounds have then been mixed into a single unity forcing the Different into union with the Same and mixing both with Existence.[32]

In this somewhat complex and confusing passage Plato is speaking of soul in its universal sense, the subject of creation. What is of particular significance is that one of its constituent elements is indivisible and unchanging, that which constitutes Form in Plato's philosophy. The Forms are unchanging, absolute, and they constitute what anything is in essence or reality. The implication is that there is a Form of soul just as there is a Form of Good, Justice, Truth and of more tangible things in the physical world. The Creator has implanted something of what constitutes Form in the universal soul, just as he has implanted intellect in soul and soul in body.

Plato then moves on from the universal soul to the individual soul which he tells us is created in the same way but with 'further dilutions'. This means that it is further removed from the perfect or the Form. The creator turns to the same bowl in which he mixed the universal soul and pours into it what is left of the former in-gredients, mixing them in the same fashion: '... only not quite so pure, but in second and third degree.'[33]

This means that no individual soul is perfect, but it also means that some souls are nearer to perfection than others in that they may possess more or less of the nature of Form, some in second and some in third degree. It is this which determines their superior or inferior potential.

Plato tells us that the souls are then allotted to stars and, mounted on their stars as if on chariots, they are shown the nature of the universe and told the laws of destiny. To ensure 'fair treatment', he says the first incarnation will be the same for all. This seems strangely contradictory since Plato has just told us that some souls have greater potential than others at the very moment of creation. This means that in their first incarnation, even if it is the same for all, some souls have a head start, and this is inconsistent with any notion of 'fair treatment'. Likewise Plato's further assertion that: '... human kind being of two sexes, the better of the two was that which in future would be called man,'[34]

It is in this first incarnation, subject to desires, pleasures and pains, that the individual souls are assessed and their future decided. Those who can master their feelings return to their native star and live an appropriately happy life. Those who fail to do so: '.... would be changed into a woman at second birth'.[35]

That woman is inferior is clear. What is also clear is the nature of her inferiority. It lies in the inability to conquer one's feelings and emotions, sensations of pleasure as well as of pain. This is reminiscent of the tripartite soul of *The Republic* where the higher element of reason must rule over the lower elements of spirit and appetite in order to be in harmony. Here, the soul in disharmony is deposited in the female body as a visible mark of its inferiority.

Later in the dialogue the relegation of a soul to a female body is expressly described as a kind of punishment. Plato tells us that the men of the first generation who lived cowardly or immoral lives were reborn in the second generation as women. The meaning of this is quite clear. However, something more interesting emerges at this point. Plato adds:

... and it was therefore at that point of time that the gods produced sexual love, constructing in us and in women a living creature itself instinct with life.[36]

This indicates that male and female do not function sexually as such until the second incarnation. It would be tempting to interpret this as meaning that there is no real male-female distinction in the first incarnation, that soul at this stage, and likewise in its pre-existence, is sex-neutral. The body, after all, in male or female form, has been created second and, we are told, is of lesser importance than soul. But this explanation will not do. It does not tell us why it is essential for the best souls to be placed in the first instance in a male receptacle, albeit one which does not initially function biologically.

To find an explanation of this we have to return to Plato's notion of Forms. The Form, the absolute standard of reality, is what anything is in a state of perfection. Examples of any entity are mere copies. What the separation of good and bad souls, and the placing of the good souls in a male body means, is that soul, in essence, or in Form, in its state of perfection, is masculine. The male body containing the superior soul is closer to the Form than is the female. It is not the soul but the body of the first incarnation which is, as far as biological function goes, sex-neutral. Its sexual function does not begin until the good and bad souls have been weeded out. But the good and the bad have, in a sense, been predetermined. Those with most of the Form are clearly more likely to lead a first earthly existence which is good.

When this first existence is completed the good souls, those which will ascend once again to the heavens, are already in male bodies, a position from which the ascent may begin. They are already the copy of perfection. Those souls which are wicked are in a female body and will suffer further earthly incarnations. Continued wrongdoing will result in their being changed into some sort of animal. The female body is the first step on a downward descent, just as the male body is the doorway through which a soul ascends to the heavens.[37]

Plato adds that there will be no respite from change and suffering until the soul allows the motion of the Same and Uniform in himself to subdue the multitude of riotous and irrational feelings which have clung to it since its association with fire, water, air and earth, and with reason once again in control, returned to its 'first and best form'.[38]

The female, then, is associated with the changing, the irrational, the imperfect. It is also associated with the physical. The soul which is descending through various stages of deterioration is being guided by those feelings which have their origin in its connection with matter. Those are the feelings which have 'clung' to it since its association with earthly life.

While there are obviously worse fates for a soul than being imprisoned in a female body, the female, nevertheless, is still one step removed from the 'best form' of soul. It is only in freeing itself from the irrational and the physical, and being once more controlled by reason, that the soul manages to return to its superior state. In other words, it regains its masculinity.

It can be seen from this that the body, though of lesser importance than the soul, is not insignificant for either male or female. The masculine body plays a part in the ascent to pure knowledge. The female body is that which houses the inferior souls incapable of making the ascent.

PLATO AND SEX UNITY THEORY

In identifying three main theories concerning gender in philosophy – sex unity, sex polarity and sex complementarity – Prudence Allen argues that the first complete foundation for sex unity theory, the notion that men and women are fundamentally the same and therefore equal, is attributable to Plato.[39]

Allen, however, relies rather too heavily on the evidence of *The Republic* to support this contention and while not dismissing the obvious inconsistencies in what Plato says about women, nevertheless decides that the development of sex unity theory is Plato's 'most significant contribution' to the theory of sex identity in philosophy. The implication is that whatever else Plato may have had to say about the matter, sex unity, as a new philosophical position developed by him, was what he really believed about men and women.[40]

Allen acknowledges that *The Timaeus* presents a contradictory picture, one of sex polarity, the belief that men and women are fundamentally different and that men are superior to women. She accepts also that *The Timaeus* was written in Plato's later period, a fact which would suggest that what he says in *The Republic* cannot be assumed to be his final word on the subject.

Allen attempts to reconcile this problem but her conclusions are deeply unsatisfactory. She argues that Plato offers a 'cosmic' theory of sex polarity in *The Timaeus* and that this enables him to explain the apparent inferiority of women in Greek society at the time. His careful arguments for sex unity in an ideal society, she claims, allow him to suggest a way of reforming society to conform better to true reality. Sex unity she sees as corresponding better to Plato's view of the way the material world ought to be.[41]

But 'true reality' for Plato is the realm of the Forms. It is the Forms which give life and meaning to his cosmic theory. If the inferiority of women in Greek society is explicable in terms of the cosmic theory, why should Plato posit a conflicting theory for men and women in the Ideal State, the state founded on Justice, itself one of the Forms? The social and political position of women, both in Greek society of the day and in the Ideal State, would be justifiably unequal to that of men from the very moment of creation as described in *The Timaeus*. Allen's argument would mean that Plato did not really believe his own cosmic theory and that true reality in his terms, reflected in the equality of male and female guardians, is what is found in *The Republic*. This is hardly credible.

Plato is quite explicit about the souls of women in *The Timaeus*. They are inferior male souls. If women are inferior to men at a spiritual level, why should Plato grant them equality in an earthly existence and invent an entirely new theoretical framework for his political theory to justify doing so?

The answer is that he does no such thing and he is not a sex unity theorist. Plato is, in fact, consistent in his view of sex identity. He is, in *The Republic* as well as in *The Timaeus*, a sex polarity theorist. For Plato men and women are fundamentally different. Women have inferior souls and unity in Plato's sex identity theory is the unity of masculinity.[42]

Where Allen's analysis of Plato's theory has gone wrong is in her misinterpretation of Plato's use of the term 'nature', which she interprets as being an earthly reflection of soul.[43] This is not the case. While soul and nature are certainly connected, as are soul and intellect, the two are not identical.

She cites first of all a passage in *The Timaeus* where Plato speaks of a 'mother receptacle' which is totally passive, and which is the recipient of all impressions. The Forms which enter into and go out of her are the likeness of eternal realities.[44] This means, says Allen, that the Earth Mother has become simply the metaphysical concept of Prime Matter. The Cosmic Father, however, is likened to the Forms.[45]

A further passage is cited in support of this argument. Plato speaks of three 'natures'. The first is that which is in the process of generation; the second, that in which generation takes place; the third, that of which the thing generated is a resemblance naturally produced. He adds:

> And we may liken the receiving principle to a mother, the source or spring to a father, and the intermediate nature to a child.[46]

Allen argues that this means Plato sees the entry of true Forms into matter as similar to the father's act of depositing the seed during sexual intercourse.[47] It is clear that Plato associated fathering with Forms, and mothering with the reception of Forms by matter. On a cosmic level, therefore, he introduces a kind of sex polarity through his subsequent affirmation of the value of Forms over matter.[48]

But she claims that an examination of *The Republic* presents a different picture. Here, in speaking of male and female 'nature' Plato comments:

> .... if the only difference apparent between them is that the female bears and the male begets, we shall not admit that this is a difference relevant for our purpose, but shall still maintain that our male and female guardians ought to follow the same occupations.[49]

Allen's interpretation of this is that woman's or man's identity comes from their mind, or soul, and not from body. Soul is an immaterial and therefore non-sexual entity.[50] Therefore, she concludes, when Plato considered men and women from the perspective of their 'real nature' he decided they were the same. It is the sexless soul and not the material body that determines the identity of man or woman.[51]

But this is a strange turnabout in Allen's own argument. For in analyzing *The Timaeus* in terms of sex polarity, she herself has acknowledged that Plato argues for sexual identity of non-material and non-bodily cosmic principle. Form is an altogether abstract and non-physical essence and it is this which Allen has maintained that Plato likens to the father; it is the notion or 'metaphysical concept' of prime matter that is likened to the mother.

In other words, immaterial and non-bodily things are still imbued with notions of gender. The soul, though immaterial, still has sexual identity. And according to Plato's cosmic theory it is the Form of soul which is masculine, it is matter which is feminine. A male body actually derives its identity, its masculinity, from the nature of its soul. Soul in its 'best form', as Plato himself has described it, is masculine. The first step on the downward descent from this superior position, it must be remembered, is for the soul to be placed in the body of a woman.

Plato actually presents a kind of sex unity in *The Timaeus*. It is not, however, unity in the sense of indicating the equality of men and women through the possession of a sexless soul. Since Plato presents the perfect soul as masculine, unity, in his eyes, is the completeness of masculinity.

Polarity is a distinction between male and female, and there is no doubt that Plato does make such a distinction. But the difference is not between male and female souls, for there is no female soul in *The Timaeus*. Souls do not polarize into male and female but into superior and inferior. The superior are deposited in male bodies associated with fathering and therefore with the 'Cosmic Father', the inferior are deposited in female bodies associate with the notion of passive 'Prime Matter'.

The feminine is an altogether different concept from soul. What is more, it stands in opposition to it and, associated with body, it is a potential contamination of the best souls, a threat to their attaining their finest form. The feminine in fact ceases to exist when the ascent to knowledge is achieved. The female represents necessity in *The Timaeus*. Woman is needed for the reproduction of the human body. But soul, in its attainment of perfection, relinquishes body and leaves it behind in its ascent to the Forms. Corruption, Plato makes clear, comes about through association with the physical.[52]

And Plato is not inconsistent in his view of the feminine in *The Republic*. Plato's assertion that women and men with 'similar natures' should do similar tasks does not automatically mean that he sees nature as emanating from soul and therefore that the souls of male and female are the same.

Plato uses the term 'nature' in different ways to mean different things. And while nature might well spring from soul or reflect something of the quality of soul, it can be shown that the two are not interchangeable.

For example, in the watchdog analogy in *The Republic* where Plato asks if there is any reason why female watchdogs should be restricted to rearing puppies, and then extends the argument to men and women, suggesting that they too should share all tasks, he acknowledges that there are great 'natural' differences between the male and the female. He makes clear, however, that in this context he is referring to their biological function. The female bears, the male begets. And he concludes that if this is the only difference it is insufficient reason to prevent them performing the same tasks. Biological 'nature', then, does not determine how one carries out particular tasks or duties.[53]

Plato goes on to say that a bald-headed and a long-haired man may have opposite natures and asks which will make the better cobbler. He admits that this question is absurd and adds:

> We never meant that natures are the same or different in an unqualified sense but only with reference to the kind of sameness or difference which is relevant to various employments. For instance, we should regard a man and a woman with medical ability as having the same nature.[54]

Nature, here, is clearly a question of ability or expertise in a given field and either men or women may possess it. One cannot even interpret nature in this context as intelligence, though it may spring from the level of intelligence possessed. It relates rather to the type of ability displayed since men and women with a similar level of intelligence might nevertheless excel in different skills. It is the similarity of expertise which constitutes nature and therefore 'sameness'.

Intelligence, in any case, is no more synonymous with soul than is nature. Intellect expresses itself through soul, but they are not one and the same. This applies also to nature when defined in terms of particular ability. Consequently, the fact that nature in such terms defies gender distinctions does not constitute evidence that the soul itself is sex-neutral.

However, when Plato describes the nature of women in terms of typical personality traits, and cites these as quarrelsomeness, emotion and ambition, and when he asserts that they are in general, in all respects, inferior to men, female nature can be seen to have taken on yet another meaning.[55] Nature here seems to indicate characteristics which can be identified as feminine as distinct from masculine.

It can be seen, then, that nature has different facets, and men and women are the same or different depending upon which aspect is being examined. Plato has made clear himself in using the ludicrous example of the bald-headed or long-haired cobbler that one cannot speak of sameness or difference in an unqualified sense.

Allen also cites *The Phaedrus* as evidence of Plato's sex unity theory. In this dialogue, she points out, the soul loses its perfection with the shedding of its wings and descends into earthly incarnations in varying degrees of wisdom. There is no mention, she says, of sex differences in the categories of lives which Plato offers, nor of why the soul should have fallen in the first place.

As far as the categories of lives are concerned this is true; they do not specifically mention sex difference. But one needs to question why this is. The categories are: a seeker after wisdom or beauty, a law-abiding monarch or warrior and commander, a man of affairs or financier, a lover of physical activity or trainer or physician, a sooth-sayer or official of the mysteries, a poet or practitioner of some imitative art, an artisan or farmer, a popular teacher or demagogue and, finally a tyrant.[56]

Given the lack of employment opportunities for women outside the home, and their very restricted role in every sense in Plato's day, one needs to enquire how many of these categories would be associated with the female at all. Even those categories which do not automatically suggest they are intended for the male of the species, and some, like 'warrior', clearly do, have this question mark hanging over them. Female poets, for example, were not entirely unknown at this time, but they were certainly rare and their existence is only known from relatively few surviving fragments. The one comparatively famous female Greek poet was Sappho, born around 612 BC, and she was an exception.

A more likely interpretation of this passage is that it does not prove that women were undifferentiated; it suggests rather that they were left entirely out of account. In fact, in all respects, the focus of attention of *The Phaedrus* is exclusively masculine. It is a dialogue which deals with loving relationships in both their physical and emotional sense. But it is clear at the outset that it is the love between a man and a boy of which Plato speaks.[57]

And it is in this dialogue that Plato tells us more about soul, most crucially about its association with body. Having indicated that a combination of soul and body is termed 'mortal', he adds that there is no reason for positing the existence of such a being who is immortal. But he goes on to say that because we have never seen or formed an adequate idea of a god, we picture him to ourselves as being the same as ourselves but immortal: ' . . . a combination of soul and body indissolubly joined for ever.'[58] What Plato is saying is that there may well be a divine body though its existence cannot be proved. He leaves the matter open with the comment: 'The existence of such beings and the use of such language about them we must leave to the will of God.'[59] But the clear implication is that if such a being exists there is a Form of body just as there is a Form of soul. It is a combination of the two which constitutes the divine. And while Plato leaves final proof of the divine to the will of God, he nevertheless goes on to argue that the earthly copy of the Form of body is to be found in the body of a young boy.[60]

What is more it is the sight of this which stimulates the soul's recollection of absolute Beauty. The divine is the combination of the masculine body and the masculine soul, those things which emulate perfection, the Form.

Plato emphasizes this in his assertion that certain souls fall to earth because they have missed most of the vision of reality while travelling in the train of the gods.[61] And Plato, in fact, does tell us why this happens. He gives a detailed account of it.

He tells us that when the soul is perfect it is winged. The function of the wings is to take what is heavy and raise it up to the region where the gods dwell. Of all things connected with the body, the wing has the greatest affinity with the divine, which is endowed with Beauty, Wisdom, Goodness and every other excellence.[62]

Excellence is the prime source of nourishment and growth of the wings but its opposite, ugliness and evil cause the wings to perish. Zeus, driving a team of winged horses, leads the gods in procession and they are followed by whoever is able and willing to follow them. Some go easily and are led to the region beyond the heavens, the abode of reality with which true knowledge is concerned, an abode which is without shape or colour, intangible but real: apprehensible by intellect which is the pilot of the soul.[63]

But the journey is not so easy for some. There are souls which have chariots driven by unruly horses. These are dragged downwards and their vision of reality is impaired. They must wait for the next circuit of the heavens to follow again in the train of the gods.

Still others have failed to follow at all and have missed the vision of reality entirely. These sink beneath the burden of forgetfulness and wrongdoing, lose their wings and sink to earth.[64]

It is therefore made quite clear why some souls lose their wings. They have missed the vision of reality and have lost sight of every excellence, including beauty. They have been tainted with ugliness and their wings have perished.

In the matter of sexual identity of the soul, however, it is not the loss of the wings which is most significant. It is its efforts to regain them. It is here that Plato makes clear that the erotic, acceptable only in a limited degree, is also acceptable only if it is of a certain kind. It is male eroticism which plays a part in the soul's attempt to regain its wings.

The entire process may take ten thousand years, but it can be shortened, Plato tells us, if it involves the love of a boy. We are not immediately told why this type of love should facilitate the attainment of excellence, merely that the search for wisdom without guile, combined with the love of a boy, helps the wings to grow again.[65]

However, Plato has already said that it is ugliness that makes the wings perish. The love of a boy, therefore, is connected with beauty. The connection, we are told, is that the sight of a beautiful boy stimulates the recollection of ideal beauty.[66]

The man who is corrupt cannot make the transition from beauty on earth to absolute beauty. He abandons himself to sensuality of one kind or another. He either wishes to beget children, 'like a four-footed beast', or he gives himself to unnatural pleasures.[67]

Now the mating and begetting of children clearly involves association with the female. It cannot be otherwise, This is, therefore, the first reference in the dialogue, albeit an implicit one, to women, and what is said of them clearly relegates them to the non-beautiful and animal aspects of life. They do not stimulate the wings to grow and the soul which is 'abandoned' to this type of union does not return to the realm of the Forms.

Only those who love a beautiful boy will regrow their wings. They are the ones who, before life have had '.... a full sight of the celestial vision.'[68] The reflection of the celestial vision on earth, therefore, is the god-like face and physical form of a young boy.

It is clear, then, that the union of the perfect soul with the perfect body, or the Form of soul and the Form of body, incorporates the idea of masculinity at every level. The Form of soul, according to *The Timaeus*, is masculine. *The Phaedrus* now tells us that the perfect body is masculine. Once again we have sex unity, but not the unity of the male and female joined in equality. What we have is the unity of all things male – soul, body, intellect and eroticism.

It is to be noted, however, that Plato also speaks of 'unnatural pleasure' and associates it with the mating and begetting of children as an abandoned form of love-making. This too must be rejected if the wings of the soul are to grow. What this obviously means is that while love between man and boy may initially stimulate the soul's ascent, there must be no unrestrained expression of physical love between them. It is clear that Plato sees this as similar to the inferior love between men and women which leads only to the begetting of children. Real knowledge is only attained with the elimination of the physical in favour of the spiritual.

Plato explains this more fully in the myth of the Charioteer and his horses. The myth represents Reason as the Charioteer with one good and beautiful horse, Spirit, and one unruly and ugly horse, Appetite. The struggle by Reason to prevent the unruly horse from dragging down the good and beautiful horse, it becomes clear, is the struggle to overcome desire, the desire for homosexual intercourse.[69]

It is obvious that physical love between a man and woman cannot be transcended in this way as it is a necessary function in the production of children. Transcendence of this kind is only possible for the male. This sheds further light on the separation of good and inferior souls into male and female bodies. Inferior souls are entrapped in a body whose primary function is physical. The best souls must not be likewise imprisoned as only they have the possibility of the heavenly union, the divine body with the divine soul.

While in *The Timaeus* Plato deals in depth with male and female at a cosmic level, he does not leave earthly existence out of account. We are told that the world is not a product of reason alone but of a combination of reason and necessity. They are not, however, equal partners. The one is subordinate to the other:

> Intelligence controlled necessity by persuading it for the most part to bring about the best result, and it was by the subordination of necessity to reasonable persuasion that the universe was constituted as it is.[70]

Intelligence, closely related to and inseparable from soul, must dominate necessity, the physical side of life. But Plato tells us something more. The Creator has made the divine with his own hand but has ordered 'his own children' to make the generation of mortals:

> They took over from him the immortal principle of soul, and, imitating him, encased it in a mortal physical globe, with the body as a whole for vehicle.[71]

As Plato expands his argument it becomes clear that the female, associated with the physical, is actually twice removed from the divine. Once, because the soul, made by the Creator's own hand, is masculine. Twice, because when the Creator's children implant the principle of soul in the skull, and then in the body, Plato tells us, a further mortal part is added.

This is the part which contains 'terrible and necessary feelings'.

These include pleasure, which Plato describes as the chief incitement to wrong; pain, which frightens us from the good; obstinate passion; and credulous hope. To this mixture are added irrational sensation and desire which shrink from nothing. Those things together give the mortal its 'indispensable equipment'.[72]

It is clear from this that it is the physical, the irrational, the passionate which constitute necessity. The necessary and mortal are linked to Prime Matter, the female. The rational, spiritual and controlled are the divine and immortal. They are associated with Form, the masculine.

It is the mortal part which men must rise above to attain the realm of reason and a heavenly existence. It is the mortal which drags souls down towards earthly existence. A final passage in *The Timaeus* bears this out. When Plato discusses fitness of mind he says we should think of the most authoritative part of our soul as the guardian spirit given by god, living in the summit of the body, which can properly be said to lift us from earth towards our home in heaven. The soul, he says, was first born in heaven and the divine part of us attaches us by the head to heaven like a plant by its roots:

> If therefore man's attention and effort is centred on appetite and ambition, all his thoughts are bound to be mortal, and he can hardly fail, in so far as it is possible, to become entirely mortal, as it is his mortal part he has increased.[73]

Men must rise above the appetitive, the ambitious, the mortal in order to reach their heavenly home. But it is clear that women have no means of making this ascent. They are, by definition, associated with everything which is mortal. Women constitute necessity in the universe. Necessity is that which men must first of all control and then transcend. It is this process of transcendence, contained within Plato's theory of love, which must be examined next.

3 The Transcendent Male

Plato's theory of love, like his theory of knowledge, rests on the notion of an ascent. Whereas knowledge is arrived at by rising up from ignorance to truth, love is achieved by means of a similar ascent from sexuality – which is mistaken for love but which, in Plato's view, is merely animal lust – to real love, which is spiritual. Like knowledge, love involves a notion of the Forms, those unchanging entities which belong in the spiritual realm. Just as there is a Form of knowledge, so also there is a Form of love, perceived only by the best souls, governed by intellect. Women, the embodiment of inferior male souls, and ruled as they are by the physical passions, have no means of making the ascent. Transcendence and gender are undeniably linked; the transcendent female does not and cannot exist. It is a contradiction in terms.

TRANSCENDENCE AND GENDER

The connection between transcendence and gender is clearly borne out by the evidence of the dialogues in which Plato expresses his theory of love, *The Phaedrus* and *The Symposium*. For while the idea of real love which appears in both seems to be masculine by virtue of the exclusion of the feminine, this is a superficial interpretation. Plato's notion of love is swaddled in layers of meaning which, once penetrated, reveal an altogether different picture. The masculine, in fact, does not simply reject, but triumphs over the feminine.

Implicit, of course, in the notion of triumph is the notion of the enemy or the alien – a threat in some sense to that which is triumphant.

That knowledge and love are linked, that there is a Form of each just as there is a Form of good, the ultimate to be achieved by intellectual ascent, is reflected in the very nature of the sexuality which is involved. In this connection Michel Foucault's description of the attainment of knowledge by means of sexual contact is particularly apt. In discussing the transformation of sex into discourse Foucault argues that in Greece truth and sex were linked, in the form of pedagogy, by the transmission of a precious knowledge from one body to another. Sex served as a medium for initiations into learning.[1]

Formal learning was, of course, available only to young men; the pedagogic process was confined to older men and young boys. If sexual activity was part of the learning process it was also an initiation to sexual union of a particular and exclusive kind. Evelyn Fox Keller's contention that Plato maps out a path to knowledge, guided by love, which is insulated from the aggression that both he and his culture associated with sensible, material and female nature, is significant, as is her conclusion that his theory is 'immune' to the subversive powers of the irrational and achieves transcendence while it remains compromised by immanence.[2]

Immunity signifies a protection against something harmful, a protection which enables the potential victim to fight back and to overcome. Plato's theory does not simply depend on the exclusion of the irrational, but on the defeat of the irrational, the victory of the rational mind over its opponent. Knowledge must not simply be separated from, but freed from, human life and physical love. Passion and flesh, associated most with the female, are those things which the masculine soul must struggle to overcome to attain once again its finest Form.

In *The Phaedrus* the love referred to is the love between man and boy. The struggle to overcome the physical is the struggle to overcome homosexual physical love. It becomes clear, however, that the reason why this type of love must be rejected is because it is seen to be tainted with the kind of unrestrained passion associated with female nature and with heterosexual intercourse. Plato tells us that the man who surrenders himself to sensuality is like a four-footed beast, eager to mate and beget children.[3] The begetting of children, necessarily the result of heterosexual intercourse, is therefore a purely animal function. Relationships between men are not superior simply by their exclusion of the feminine, but by their distinct qualitative difference from relationships between men and women. The latter are depicted here as bestial, if essential.

Likewise, in *The Symposium* the conflict between transcendence and immanence can be seen to be gender-related. Once again, where meaningful love is spoken of, it is the love between two males. Diotima, the priestess, tells Socrates that the object of love is to procreate and bring forth in beauty. Procreation is the object of beauty because it is the nearest thing to perpetuity and immortality that a mortal being can attain. Love is love of immortality as well as of the good.[4]

This appears, at first sight, to bestow an enhanced status on procreation. There are, however, different kinds of procreation. Not all of them lead to immortality. Diotima gives an explanation which is worth quoting at length:

> Those whose creative instinct is physical have recourse to women, and show their love in this way believing that by begetting children they can secure an immortal and blessed memory hereafter forever; but there are some whose creative desire is of the soul and who long to beget spiritually, not physically, the progeny which it is the nature of the soul to create and bring to birth. If you ask what that progeny is, it is wisdom and virtue in general. . . .[5]

This clearly relegates women to the realm of the physical, and physical love with women has only one purpose: the begetting of human children. Immortality is not to be had through physical reproduction but by the attainment of wisdom and virtue. This is achieved intellectually. It is the triumph of mind over body, and here Plato explicitly depicts woman as body. It is interesting, too, that this pronouncement should come from the mouth of one of the few women who appear indirectly in the dialogues; but more of that later.

For the moment, one may say that the fact that Plato uses sexual language, specifically the language of reproduction, to explain the attainment of wisdom does not enhance the status of body or of female. Plato is speaking of a superior, non-bodily type of begetting. He is speaking of creation, not reproduction. Women reproduce body, men create wisdom. Creation of this sort is external to body and not all men are capable of it. Those who are not 'have recourse to women'. Women, within a heterosexual relationship, serve one purpose, have one destiny. Women are, as Plato has depicted them in *The Timaeus*, 'Necessity'.[6] Only homosexual love is the starting-point for the ascent to philosophy.

Saxonhouse argues, to the contrary, that the relationship between the intellectual and bodily processes of labour and birth ties Socrates and his activities to biological woman.[7] She maintains that for Socrates the advantages of strength and weakness and the apparent disadvantages of reproductive responsibilities have no effect on the activity of philosophy. According to Saxonhouse, politics, for the Greeks before Aristotle, entailed the use of body in war; philosophy, as its opposite, did not require the body. By introducing the female into his political community, she claims, Socrates is asserting the superiority of philosophy over politics; by bringing the female into public life, he is suggesting the irrelevance of the body. For Socrates, the activity of philosophy is a life-giving force which parallels the creation of life.[8]

But *The Symposium* makes clear that the activity of philosophy does not parallel the creation of life but, rather, supersedes it. The creation of human children is an altogether inferior form of procreation. And while Plato does allow women into his political community in *The Republic*, he stresses that men are far better at most things – with the exception of domestic tasks like cooking,where a woman would be laughed at if a man did them better.[9] The argument is the same with regard to procreation. In its ideal form this is spiritual, not physical. Consequently, men are superior in this, as in everything else.

The notion that physical procreation is inferior is repeated in *The Menexenus* where Aspasia, in her funeral oration, points out that the country is the true mother of man. She has provided his nourishment. Aspasia adds:

> ... it is not the country that imitates the woman in the matter of conception and birth, but the woman the country.[10]

Women are once again seen to provide a humble version of something which has a much finer form.

The basis of this superior form of birth, however, is still physical. It begins with love between two males. Since all physical love must be transcended because of its association with inferior and potentially corrupting flesh, homosexual eros is also problematic for Plato. In its physical expression it resembles the love between man and woman. It is still of the flesh.

Keller acknowledges this and comments that just as mind remains embedded in matter, so even homosexual eros continues to reside in bodies. The love of man for man remains inextricably compounded of bodily and spiritual desire, in ways that constantly threaten the division between transcendence and immanence. She argues that for Plato the surrender to physical desire reduces homosexual eros to the status of heterosexual or animal desire.[11]

In other words, Plato believes that when men have physical relationships with other men or boys they merely simulate the inferior union of men and women. Such a union has its own purpose – the production of children. It does not inspire real love nor stimulate the ascent to philosophy. Consequently, men must rise above physical love with each other in the same way that they must rise above the physical desire they have for women. Men must reject and overcome the physical, the flesh, the feminine.

HOMOSEXUALITY IN ATHENIAN CULTURE

That homosexuality was a part of classical Athenian culture is well documented. What is often not fully appreciated, however, is the range and complexity of such relationships, also that they did not always enjoy unqualified social approval, and on occasion excited not only disapproval but legal penalty. The problematic nature of certain types of relationships between males has prompted Hans Kelson to argue that Plato was, in fact, impelled to sublimate his eros primarily because it was in conflict with the moral and legal views of the Athenian society of his time. He adds that the belief that pederasty was quite widespread, and hence not morally repudiated, is quite incorrect.[12]

In fact, only for the Dorian State has it been proved that homosexual practices between men and youths were openly acknowledged, and then only by an elite of nobles. At the same time there were ancient laws which punished sexual love of boys with death and ostracism.[13]

Conflicting views on pederasty are evident in the dialogues. For while there are sufficient references to such relationships, social disapproval is also expressed. For example, in *Lysis* when Hippothales blushes to be asked which handsome young man is his favourite, it is because of his erotic feelings for the boy. Socrates is not slow to pick up the signals and to tell Hippothales that he can see that he is not just in love but that he is 'already far gone in it'.[14]

The fact that Socrates uses the term 'in love', and that Hippothales blushes, indicates that it is not simply friendship or brotherly love to which Socrates refers. It is clear also that in a situation where Socrates and his friends talk, man to man, such feelings may be discussed freely, albeit with the degree of embarrassment which customarily accompanies such intimate confidences.

But in *The Phaedrus* when Socrates speaks of the love of an older man for a boy he comments that the lover would be happy for the boy to be without father, mother, kindred or friends:

.... because their disapproval is likely to prevent him from deriving the highest enjoyment from the liaison.[15]

This indicates that Athenian families placed definite limitations on
how far relationships between older men and young boys should
go. While an association with an older and learned mentor may
be acceptable, even desirable at a certain level, the idea being
the education of the youth, a full sexual relationship was clearly
frowned on.

How the law viewed pederasty certainly varied from place to place.
In some states, for example Sparta, boy-loving was accepted even
in law. In Athens, however, the law discouraged it.[16]

However, while homosexuality itself was not actually against the
law in Athens, certain homosexual practices were. K.J. Dover points
out that there were penalties for male prostitution, the severity of
which depended upon the nature of the charge. As evidence for
this he cites the prosecution of Timarchus, pointing out that the
text of the trial shows that other aspects of homosexuality were
referred to openly and clearly incurred no penalty.[17]

However, Aeschines' *Speech Against Timarchus* indicates that while
certain practices were known to go on, they were not considered
acceptable. Speaking of the legislator, Aeschines says he enacted
laws for 'unbecoming things' known to go on in the city. This refers to the corruption of youth by older men, and the penalties do
not fall on the youths who are seen to be the victims of the crime,
but on those seen to be the perpetrators – the older men. Aeschines
makes clear that if any boy is let out for hire as a prostitute, whether
it be by father or brother or uncle or guardian, prosecution is not
to lie against the boy himself: '... but against the man who let
him out for hire and the man who hired him'.[18] While this applies
only to prostitution, the implication is that youths, generally speaking,
would usually not be willing participants, in such arrangements.
They were being abused and corrupted by the older men who were
obliging them to assume a passive role – the role of the female.

It is Dover's contention that this is how such relationships were
customarily depicted. The older man, the *erastēs*, pursued, the boy,
the *erōmenos*, made a concession of sexual favours to a worthy
erastēs. Young men were not depicted as enjoying sexual intercourse
as women were.[19]

There are passages in the dialogues where this hierarchical arrangement is borne out. In *Lysis*, Socrates scolds Hippothales for

writing songs in honour of his boy before he has actually won him. When a man praises and compliments handsome boys, he maintains, they become filled with pride and conceit and they become harder to catch. Socrates cautions that any man who knows what's what when it comes to love does not praise the boy he's in love with until he's caught him.[20]

The notion of the reluctant youth also sheds further light on an encounter between Alcibiades and Socrates in *The Symposium*. Alcibiades approaches Socrates telling him he is the only lover worthy of him and offering to comply with his desires in this respect.[21] Alcibiades is humiliated by Socrates' rejection of him, though Socrates' behaviour does not come of repugnance but restraint and, he maintains, the experience of age. He tells Alcibiades:

> A man's mental vision does not begin to be keen until his physical vision is past its prime, and you are far from reaching that point.[22]

While Alcibiades is young, his physical desires still keen, he is supposed, as the *erōmenos*, to yield only reluctantly to a lover. Alcibiades' humiliation springs from the fact that he has made the initial approach himself, and been rejected. He describes his confused state of mind as being, on the one hand, slighted, and on the other in awe of Socrates' restraint. Refusal of this kind is obviously rare and Alcibiades admits to a reverence for Socrates' character, his self-control and courage: 'I had met a man whose like for wisdom and fortitude I could never have expected to encounter.'[23] Alcibiades has learned a lesson in love from Socrates. The spiritual side of love outstrips physical gratification. This type of love is, however, exclusively masculine. Alcibiades has debased himself by behaving like a woman in attempting to seduce Socrates into physical love-making.

Dover points out that a study of vase paintings reveals that where they depict sexual intercourse from the rear, it is always between men and women. Where face-to-face intercourse takes place it is between two males. The intercrural mode, he says, is 'normal' when the sexual object is male, but unknown when it is female.[24]

Dover's interpretation of this is that intercourse between men and women placed women in a subordinate position. The love between man and boy, where both were of the same class, was a love between equals. He maintains that there was a common Greek belief that women lacked the moral insight and firmness of purpose which allowed men to resist certain temptations. Men had no inclination to homosexual submission.[25]

Homosexual desire, then, took on different meanings depending upon which role, active or passive, was adopted by the parties concerned. The passive role in male homosexual relationships was associated with femininity and was thereby seen to be the role of the inferior. The importance of the hierarchical structure in male-male relationships and the significance of passivity in social as well as personal terms, is also discussed by John Winkler who argues that the fundamental protocols concerning men's sexual behaviour in classical Athens are personified in the figure of the hoplite, a citizen soldier, wealthy enough to provide himself with a set of armour, and the kinaidos, a socially and sexually deviant male.[26]

The significance of these images, for Winkler, lies in the fact that the kinaidos constituted the anti-type of masculinity. It was a figure of fun, or alternatively, the object of reproach.[27]

In other words, the kinaidos, a kind of caricature, was not one with which the respectable and respected Athenian male would wish to be associated. Once again, the reluctance, or at the very least, feigned reluctance, of the youth is significant. Young men might be involved in relationships which required them to bestow sexual favours but not in such a way that these would cast them in the role of kinaidos, the effeminate man.

Citing the Athenian laws which were not framed in terms of sexual deviance, but in terms of prostitution, Winkler sees the kinaidos as constituting a 'scare-image', one which represents the shaming of one's integrity as a male citizen by hiring out one's body for another man's use. The shame involved lies in the fact that the passive role in sexual encounters is associated with femininity.[28]

Relationships between men and boys, then, can only be purified by the boys' disinclination to the physical penetration of another man, but their willingness, nevertheless, to show gratitude for their education. The boys are not prostituted, for no money changes hands. Payment in kind is offered for an initiation to a world of rational thought and knowledge. It is, as Foucault has described it, the passing of knowledge from one body to another.

Alcibiades is explicit about this. He tells his audience that his object in offering Socrates his favours was that he would be able by this means to 'find out all that Socrates knew'.[29]

But in other circumstances, between other sorts of partners, where money and not knowledge was the accepted currency in the sexual exchange, submission to sexual penetration effectively constituted the forfeiture of one's citizenship. David Halperin, describing this as the surrender of one's phallus, the discarding of the marker of one's socio-sexual precedence, concludes that it was the worst degradation that a citizen could suffer:

.... equivalent to voluntary effeminization'.[30]

Women in classical Athens, typically in the passive and subordinate role, always dominated by men in physical relationships, were thereby not seen as equals. Men who assumed the passive role in homosexual encounters were degraded by virtue of the association of sexual passivity with femininity. Women, by their acceptance, and enjoyment, of the subordinate position were, in Socrates' view, incapable of the higher form of love to which he alludes in his rejection of Alcibiades and which draws a distinction between the mental and the physical. Physical love, which threatens the masculinity of either or both male partners involved, must ultimately be rejected altogether. Such love is dangerous. It is dangerous to the *erōmenos* who must adopt the inferior feminine role, and to the *erastēs* who is similarly tainted by association with femininity.

Socrates rejects Alcibiades, not because he finds him unattractive, but because he has risen above the temptation of the physical in favour of something finer. He has also protected the younger man, who has freely offered himself, from assuming the role of *kinaidos* or from voluntary effeminization.

This rejection constitutes what Kelson has termed the 'sublimation of Plato's eros'. Plato justifies the attraction of men for boys by creating for it a spiritual purpose. His attitude to homosexual relationships becomes clearer in a further examination of homosexuality in the dialogues.

HOMOSEXUALITY IN THE PLATONIC DIALOGUES

In *The Republic* Plato makes clear that sexual relationships between his male Guardians will be regulated most stringently. The Guardians will mate only at mating festivals and the occasion will be one of utmost solemnity. It must be noted, however, that the restrictions placed upon physical love are even more severe for love between men and boys than they are for love between men and women. Socrates stipulates that a lover may touch and kiss his boyfriend only as a father might kiss and touch his son. Nothing more must take place, otherwise he will be thought a man of no taste or education.[31]

This is an important prohibition because the regulation of sexual intercourse between men and women also has the practical purpose of providing the ruling elite with the best children. This is a necessary, albeit animal, process. The Guardian class must be repopulated. Obviously, this is not a consideration where physical relationships between men and boys are concerned, and while Plato has made clear that appetites, including sexual appetites, must be kept in check, there is no suggestion that this means total self-denial. Spirit and reason, once they have been trained to perform their proper function, must be put in charge of appetite, which Plato believes is naturally insatiable. Reason and spirit must prevent it from taking its fill of the so-called pleasures.[32]

This means that appetite, though it must not be satiated, may be satisfied up to a point. Plato tells us that when male and female Guardians are past the age for breeding they may mate as they please, except where the relationship would be incestuous.[33]

Yet this freedom is not allowed the male Guardians in relation to other men or younger boys. Since there is no danger here of the production of inferior offspring, Plato clearly has other reasons for the restriction.

The same ban on homosexuality appears in *The Laws* where it is to have the further sanction of religion: '. . . . if the rule is given sufficient backing, it will get a grip on every soul and intimidate it into obeying the established laws.'[34]

Clearly, then, the restriction on homosexuality is of particular importance when Plato considers the need to use what he himself calls intimidation to implement it. Earlier in the dialogue he has indicated that this law is created because in homosexual relations the human race is deliberately murdered.[35]

What this means, of course, is that this kind of sexual intercourse cannot produce children and, consequently, if only homosexual relationships existed within society then the race would die out. This seems a practical rather than a moral justification. Indeed, no mention at all is made of the morality of such relationships. It is also, however, a very unsatisfactory justification. Legalized homosexual love would surely be unlikely to put an end to all heterosexual relationships, and as long as homosexual and heterosexual love co-existed in society there would be no threat to the human race.

It follows that Plato's restrictions on homosexuality are for other reasons than the practical considerations of everyday life such as reproduction. Important as this is in Plato's ideal state, the prohibition he places on physical love between men is not concerned with procreation. Plato not only recognizes the strength of homosexual eros; he sees danger in its expression in physical form, the form which pulls the best souls downwards towards the earthly rather than the spiritual.

The fact that the rules concerning homosexual love are so stringent indicates also Plato's fear that they will be the more difficult to enforce. Winkler argues that in *The Laws* Plato attempted to create a social order which would conform to 'nature'. To do so would require a restructuring of common belief and practice which would place pederasty on the same level as incest, so that everyone would acquire a horror of it. He adds, however:

> ... what should stand out about Plato's text is the despair there felt about the impossibility, almost inconceivability, of the project.[36]

Winkler concludes that the project in *The Laws* was a 'thought experiment' which went against the grain of the values, practices and debates of Plato's society.[37]

Physical relationships between men and women cannot, of course, be totally forbidden, though certain sorts may be, and Plato explicitly prohibits incestuous ones even when the Guardians' mating years are over. However, in their prime, Guardian women must fulfill their traditional role as childbearers if the Guardian class is to be repopulated. While mating of this sort cannot be eliminated, it can be curtailed and solemnized by religious festival to attempt to remove it from any notion of personal enjoyment, fulfilment or lustful abandon. Homosexual relationships which do not produce children, and are therefore solely for the purpose of physical gratification, must be eliminated completely. Plato's attempt to release men from the power of excessive physical pleasure is an attempt to free the mind from what Keller has termed 'the subversive powers of the irrational'.[38]

When Plato allows male and female Guardians to mate as they please once they are beyond childbearing years, it is not because he sees any higher significance in physical love between men and women once it is freed from the danger of producing inferior offspring. He simply acknowledges the power of all physical attraction. He tells us that when men and women mix freely in their physical exercise their natural instincts will 'necessarily' lead them to have sexual intercourse. The necessity will be sexual and not mathematical but, as Glaucon points out: '... sex is perhaps more effective than mathematics when it comes to persuading or driving the common man to do anything.'[39] The necessity is likewise recognized when Plato makes provision for certain young men to sleep more frequently with women as a reward for distinguished service.[40] That this is a mere pretext for the production of the best children will be unknown to the men and women concerned. They will be aware only of the reward. But the fact that it is presented as a reward in the first place indicates Plato's awareness of the pull of physical attractions.

The Philosopher Kings of the ruling class, however, will be those who have entirely freed themselves from physical desire. Only they can make the ascent to pure knowledge. Not all Guardians will become Philosopher Kings. Only those who have shown themselves to have the best souls have perceived Truth. They are the ones who must be forced back into the cave of ignorance to do their duty as rulers. They have passed all practical and intellectual tests and have been: '... made to lift their mind's eye to look at the source of light, and see the good itself.'[41]

From this they can take a pattern for ordering their own life as well as that of society. They would, of course, not choose to go back to the cave but must do so out of necessity.

Those who still desire physical intercourse may mate as they please at a certain age because they are the ones who, in any case, do not have the best souls and will not become rulers. Since women have inferior souls to start with, this will automatically apply to all Guardian women, though Plato implies otherwise. Men and women beyond the age for producing children may be accorded the satisfaction they desire without threat to the foundations of the state since this is a matter for the rulers only, and without threat to the pure stock of Guardian children.

Homosexual love, however, must always be curtailed because it stands at the outset on a different plane. Should it be indulged in to any great extent, it is in danger of losing its way and missing the path to eternal love which is spiritual and, as the product of the union of the best souls, masculine.

It should be noted too that when Plato speaks of homosexuality in *The Republic* he speaks of the relationship as being restricted to the affection of father and son. This indicates that the couples concerned will most usually be older men and youths. Therefore, once again, the status of the Athenian male is of importance. The older man, still desirous of sexual intercourse, and therefore not a philosopher as a philosopher would have left this behind, is to be prevented from corrupting youth. He is to be prevented from subjecting them to an association which would involve, to an extent, their effeminization. He may mate with women as he pleases. There is no danger of corruption where his partner already belongs inescapably in the physical world. Young men must mate with women at mating festivals only, and are forbidden from having intercourse with men so that they may have a chance of transcendence, the chance to see Goodness and Truth, the chance to be Philosopher Kings.

G. Lowes Dickinson has commented that the phrase 'Platonic love' is seldom used in the sense that Plato intended. He was not thinking, says Dickinson, of love without sex feeling, a mere comradeship. He was thinking of a passion which should transform itself in the better and nobler instances into objects more and more public and disinterested: '. . . . until it should lose, or rather find, itself in direct apprehension of a higher world.'[42]

Love with women, rooted in the physical and linked to the animal process of reproduction, does not constitute real or Platonic love.

THE PHAEDRUS AND THE THEORY OF LOVE

It is in *The Phaedrus* that the internal struggle associated with homosexual eros, and the attainment of true love which constitutes the triumphant conclusion to that struggle, is given its most vivid expression. In this dialogue Socrates' speech on love relates directly to the love of man for boy and to how this should be given expression.

The Phaedrus begins with Socrates and Phaedrus discussing a speech of Lysias, a famous Attic orator. Lysias has argued that it is better for a boy to yield to a non-lover than to someone who is genuinely in love with him. Socrates is persuaded to make a speech of his own on the same theme. However, convinced by a supernatural sign that he has blasphemed, he makes a second contradictory speech.

Socrates' first speech give the first indication of the importance of love. For while he has agreed to speak on the same theme as Lysias, he does not, in fact, argue the cause of the non-lover at all. Instead, he maintains that a handsome youth in his tale is pursued by a 'subtle' person, no less in love that his other admirers, but who has persuaded him that he is not in love.[43] This, of course, is very different from a 'non-lover' and tells us clearly that however the relationship is pursued, love is an indispensable factor.

Socrates then questions what love is. Everyone, he says, will admit that it is a kind of desire. But since one does not have to be in love to desire what is beautiful, a further distinction must be made.

There are, he says, two ruling principles whose guidance men follow. One is a desire for pleasure that is innate; the other is a conviction to aim at excellence. These two principles are sometimes in agreement, sometimes at variance. The conviction which impels us towards excellence is rational, and the power by which it masters us is called self-control. The desire which drags us towards pleasure is irrational, and when it gets the upper hand in us it is called excess.[44]

Socrates maintains that there is an obvious conclusion. It is this: when the irrational desire that prevails over the conviction that aims at right is directed at pleasure derived from beauty, and in the case of physical beauty, it is powerfully reinforced by the appetites which are akin to it, so that it emerges victorious: ' . . . it takes its name from the very power with which it is endowed and is called eros or passionate love.'[45]

This means that passionate love is irrational. What is more, when a lover is in the grip of this kind of passion he will make oaths and promises which he later cannot fulfil. He will be taken to task by the boy because the boy did not realize at the start that it is far better to yield to a non-lover who is in his sober senses than to a lover who from the very nature of things is bound to be out of his mind.[46] Socrates concludes that for the lover there is only the satisfaction of an appetite, like the appetite for food. Lovers lust for boys, he says, as wolves lust for lambs.[47]

However, it must be remembered that the 'non-lover' here means no such thing. The non-lover is, in fact, as Socrates has told us, the lover who is 'subtle' and who pretends not to be in love, with all the restrained behaviour that this would require. The distinction that Plato draws is not that between one who loves and one who does not. The tension between his two guiding principles does not preclude erotic love. Rather it is the struggle between those who show restraint and those who are abandoned where the passions are concerned. Love is not absent when the aim for excellence wins the day, but it is experienced in an entirely different way from the wolf-like satisfaction of appetite which Socrates has described.

Socrates' supernatural sign now paves the way for his second speech. He decides that he has sinned and blasphemed in representing love as something evil. While a lover may be mad, his madness might come as a gift from heaven, in which case it cannot be evil. Madness, he maintains, is a nobler thing than sober sense: '. . . . madness comes from God, whereas sober sense is merely human.'[48]

However, divine madness notwithstanding, the notion of a struggle between good and bad persists. Socrates explains this by means of the myth of the winged charioteer whom he compares with the human soul. Horses and charioteers of the gods, he tells us, are all good. But in other beings there is a mixture of good and bad. This mixture Socrates likens to two horses, one good and noble, the other the opposite. The charioteer is in charge of them.

Socrates tells us that the soul which is perfect and winged moves on high and governs all creation, but the soul which has shed its wings falls to earth where it encounters solid matter. It puts on an earthly body and becomes mortal. The inferior nature of body is at once clear. It is on the loss of its perfection, its wings, that the soul enters body. Body and bodily functions, which Plato sees as animal and gross and which he associates with the female, are imperfect and incomplete.

Socrates tells us that it is the function of the wing to take what is heavy and raise it up to the region above where the gods dwell. It has the greatest affinity with the divine which is endowed with beauty, wisdom and every other excellence. These qualities are the prime source of nourishment and growth to the wings of the soul, but their opposites, such as ugliness and evil, cause the wings to perish.[49] The clear implication is that it is body and anything associated with it which is ugly and destructive because the winged soul is linked to the divine.

The struggle between good and evil, according to Socrates, is greater for some than for others. Obviously this means that those with better souls find the ascent to the divine easier to negotiate than those with inferior souls. Souls which are more in tune with the divine than with the earthly will arrive at their goal with less struggle and agony. Socrates explains that this is because the horse with the vicious nature, if he has not been well broken in, drags his driver down by throwing all his weight in the direction of the earth: '. . . . supreme then is the agony of the struggle that awaits the soul.'[50]

The struggle is between good and evil, between the earthly and the divine, the spiritual and the physical. Those who are immortal, says Socrates, will stand on the back of the universe, carried round by its revolutions and contemplating what lies outside the heavens, for it is there that reality and knowledge are to be found: '. . . apprehensible only by intellect which is the pilot of the soul.'[51]

Those whose souls cannot reach the pinnacle have no vision of reality and are left with mere opinion. They will, however, still be eager to make the ascent. For in the train of the gods, some will have attained a vision of truth and will remain unscathed until the next circuit.

Those who have failed to grasp some vision of reality will lose their wings and fall to earth. They will enter into human bodies, but of different sorts depending upon their worth. Much depends upon their first life on earth. In subsequent incarnations a soul's fate depends on the goodness or badness of a previous life. Significantly, homosexual love can help determine the goodness of a life. Socrates tells us that it takes so long for the wings of the soul to grow again that an individual soul does not return to the heavens for ten thousand years. But there is an exception to this. It does not apply to the soul of one who has sought after wisdom 'without guile' or whose love for a boy has been combined with such a search.[52]

Not only is homosexual eros at the heart of this but it is of a particular kind – that between the *erastēs* and the *erōmenos*. It is a relationship which is already governed by conventions which involve a degree of restraint in terms of its physical manifestation. While love is a crucial element in the spiritual ascent, it is love experienced and expressed in the right way. A vital part of the experience is that it is between two males, but two males who stand in a particular relationship to one another – an older man and a young boy. It is a relationship which involves pursuit on the one hand and reluctance, followed by compliance and concessions, on the other.

It is this encounter which leads to the attainment of philosophy and the journey of 10,000 years, to which Plato refers, becoming shorter. Socrates also tells us that such souls, if they choose the life of the philosopher three times successively, regain their wings in the third period of a thousand years, and in the three-thousandth year they win their release.[53]

All other souls are brought to judgement at the end of their lives and either borne aloft by justice to receive the rewards they have earned in a good life or to a place of punishment beneath the earth to expiate their sins. In the thousandth year both sorts will begin the next cycle of life and death. Truth, according to Socrates, is perceived only by those who can understand the notion of universals and arrive by use of reason at an idea of unity.

Such a process is simply the recollection of those things which the soul once perceived when it was journeying with the gods. That is why, Socrates maintains, it is right that the soul of the philosopher alone should regain its wings, because it is the soul of the philosopher which dwells in memory upon the things which the gods themselves dwell upon.[54]

But if, as part of the search for philosophy, love must be experienced only with another male, only with a young boy, it is clear that no philosopher will be female. Bearing in mind that it is only souls which have lost their perfection to begin with which find themselves in human bodies, there are clearly varying degrees of imperfection. The lesser the degree of imperfection, the more likely it is that a soul will find itself in a male body from which it is possible to make the ascent to the heavens again. The more imperfect the soul, the more likely is it to be housed in a female body, relegated forever to the endless cycle of life and death.

Socrates depicts the philosopher as standing apart from other men and drawing upon himself the accusation of madness. But this madness occurs, he maintains, when a man is reminded of true beauty by the sight of beauty on earth. The philosopher grows his wings and endeavours to fly upwards. This, he says, is the best of all forms of divine possession, both for the subject and his 'associate', for it is when he is touched by this madness that the man who is so aroused by beauty in others is called a lover.[55]

However, this passage follows on from Socrates' contention that the search for philosophy may be combined with the love of a boy. So the 'associate' to whom he refers is male. The love aroused by physical beauty in others is, therefore, the love aroused by the beauty of a young male body. Whatever the divine Form of beauty, its earthly like is only to be found in the love of one male for another. Its beginning on earth is the sight of the human form which, in Plato's view is a mere copy of the eternal. If it is only in an all-male relationship that the soul recollects that real beauty exists, it is obvious that it is the male body which is the copy of the Form. Erotic love between men and women does not carry any reminder of absolute beauty, nor is its function to restore the soul to its heavenly abode. Love of this sort is rooted firmly in the body and on earth, its purpose is physical procreation.

Socrates is quite explicit about this. He says that the man who has been corrupted does not quickly make the transition from beauty on earth to absolute beauty. When he sees beauty on earth he does not recognize it but:

> surrenders himself to sensuality and is eager like a four-footed beast to mate and beget children, or in his addiction to wantonness feels no fear or shame in pursuing a pleasure which is unnatural.[56]

Plato clearly has a distaste for the physical act of childbearing. In *The Republic* he will not even have such things represented in drama. Childbearing is a purely animal process, and here in *The Phaedrus* mating with females and the begetting of children are relegated to the gross and ugly aspects of earthly life which cannot be revered. What is more, not only is the female body not reminiscent of real beauty, it represents a kind of physical decoy which lures those of a less philosophical soul away from the true path to love and knowledge.

Significantly, however, Plato also condemns the 'pleasure which is unnatural'. Clearly not every aspect of homosexual love is beautiful either, and the growth of the wings cannot be associated with anything that is animal and ugly, for such things cause the wings to perish and die.

Socrates has to make clear what kind of homosexual eros promises higher rewards. It is obviously the kind which will promote the regrowth of the wings. He explains that for those who recognise beauty on earth in the god-like face or physical form which truly reflects beauty – in other words in the physical appearance of a young man – there is a softening of the passages from which the feathers grow. Nourishing moisture falls upon the stump of each feather and the surface of the soul swells and strives to grow from its root. It is in a state of ferment and throbbing.[57]

In this heavily erotic passage the notion of pain and conflict associated with love is evident. The terms which Plato uses, 'ferment and throbbing', are those which denote physical and sexual sensation. For it must be remembered that while it is the soul to which Plato refers, it is the soul entrapped in human body, in one of its earthly incarnations. It is, as Keller has argued, a mind which remains embedded in matter. Homosexual eros continues to reside in human bodies.[58] The conflict, therefore, between the spiritual and the physical, the transcendent and the immanent has begun.

It is Socrates' belief that a lover spends his time on earth worshipping the particular god whom he loves. There is no room for jealousy and mean spite, the lover's whole effort being concentrated upon leading the object of his love into the closest possible conformity with himself and the god he worships.[59]

This bears out Dover's contention that the *erōmenos* did not choose sexual submission, but granted favours to a certain kind of lover. The picture Plato presents here is of a young boy being treated like a god, given his initiation to philosophy within a relationship which, in itself, is seen to be divine. It is neither ordinary nor base as is the relationship between men and women which causes men to behave like 'four-footed beasts'.[60] True, its nature is still partly physical, but from physical beginnings it aspires to something higher than human procreation, and it is this which distinguishes it from other sexual relationships.

Socrates describes the union further by returning to the myth of the charioteer and the horses. The soul, he says, is divided into three elements. These elements are likened to the charioteer and his two horses. One horse is good and beautiful, thirsts for honour and is tempered by restraint. The other horse is ugly and bad. It is crooked, lumbering and ill-made, and it is scarcely controllable even with a whip.[61]

This is consistent with Plato's description of the soul in *The Republic*. The tripartite soul has three elements: reason, spirit and appetite. Reason must rule, with spirit as its support, and both must keep appetite in subjection. Reason in *The Phaedrus* is represented by the charioteer with spirit as the good horse and appetite the bad horse that must be held in check.

In the case of the charioteer and his horses the significance of spirit and restraint are explained in relation to love and beauty. When the charioteer sees his beloved he feels desire but the obedient horse, constrained by shame, holds him back from springing upon the boy. The other horse, however, rushes forward, driving the charioteer to approach the youth and speak of physical love. The charioteer and the good horse at first resist but they are forced, because the bad horse will give them no peace, to yield and advance. The vision of the beloved dazzles, and the driver remembers absolute beauty which he sees again not only enthroned in a holy place but, significantly, attended by chastity. Absolute beauty, then, the Form, of which the boy's beautiful body is the reminder, is chaste; it does not entail the physical which the bad horse symbolizes. It is important to note, however, that it is only through the temptation of the evil horse that the dazzling vision is attained. Desire serves its purpose, it is part of the process. But desire must be overcome.

Abandoned lovemaking of a physical nature is to be feared, and the charioteer falls upon his back in fear and awe at the thought of it. In doing so he pulls both horses down upon their haunches. The good horse gives way willingly but the lustful horse resists with all his strength.[62]

The struggle to restrain the unruly horse is the struggle to resist physical intercourse. This, of course, can only be resisted where the relationship is between two men. It can never be completely resisted between a man and a woman. Even within the Guardian class male and female must reproduce, although Plato attempts to regiment the process to the extent that the personal element is eliminated and only service to the state remains. He cannot, however, ignore the strength of physical desire, as his stated intention to use sexual intercourse as a reward for certain Guardians indicates.

Plato acknowledges the power – an even greater power than the desire of man for woman, since its origin is divine – of the desire of man for man, in particular of the older man for the younger. But in this case, whatever the strength of feeling, desire must be overcome, otherwise there will be no ascent to real knowledge which that very desire is intended to stimulate. Should the charioteer succumb to the wicked horse he will be victim to his appetitive elements; he will show himself capable only of the kind of love which a man can have for a woman, an inferior and earthly kind of love.

It must be noted, however, that the lustful horse is not easily subdued. The attempt is made again and again to entice the charioteer and the good horse to approach the boy. The driver continues to pull the rein, ever more violently, until finally, after several repetitions, the wicked horse abandons its lustfulness:

> ... and when he catches sight of the loved one is ready to die of fear. So at last it comes about that the soul of the lover waits upon his beloved in reverence and awe.[63]

Fear attends the outcome, and it would be tempting to draw an obvious conclusion: that Plato associated all erotic love with wickedness, fear and guilt, that he wished to rid his society of this kind of love at least to the extent that it was practically possible to do so. The breeding arrangements in *The Republic* would make perfect sense in this light. The act of sexual intercourse must take place stripped of passion and lust, sanctified by religious festival, and with one object in mind, the production of the best possible children. The prohibition placed upon homosexual love would also be consistent with this view.

But such a conclusion is inadequate. It does not fully explain the role of erotic love between men in the ascent to knowledge. This type of love is quite distinct from any other and it is a vital aspect of the ascent. It cannot be eliminated from the process. It must first be experienced and then transcended. Significantly, the myth of the charioteer does not end with the submission of the unruly horse. The erotic is not, and cannot be, dismissed from the ascent.

The beloved, treated like a god, feels kindly towards his admirer; he realizes that no other affection he receives can compare with that which a god has inspired. He returns the affection and feels the longing that the lover has felt for him. The wings of the beloved begin to grow though he cannot explain what is happening to him. Socrates explains: '. . . he does not realise that he is seeing himself in his lover as in a glass.'[64]

There is a narcissistic element in this which places Plato's contempt of the love of men for women in clear perspective. Just as the lover admires a boy, besotted by the beauty of youth, a reminder of true beauty, so the boy feels love through the reflection of himself in his lover's eyes. There is an identification with one another of a type which cannot exist between two people of the opposite sex.

The youth now feels the desire for physical contact, and ultimately wants to share his lover's bed. It is not long before these desires are fulfilled in action. The lover's unruly horse has a word to say to the charioteer. It claims to be allowed a little enjoyment for all that it has suffered. The boy's unruly horse has nothing to say, and simply wishes to demonstrate affection, refusing no favour to his lover. However, the good horse in the boy's soul provides the moderating influence.[65]

Consequently, if the higher elements in their minds prevail and guide them into a life which is strictly devoted to the pursuit of wisdom, they will pass their time on earth in happiness and harmony. Their souls will be at peace when they have subdued the seeds of vice and set free the part of the soul in which virtue has its birth.[66]

A compromise has been reached. Virtue triumphs over vice and does not allow sexual appetite to be satiated. But erotic love claims a little enjoyment. At the end of their lives the lovers are borne aloft by their regrown wings and, after three such lives, they are released from the life cycle.[67]

It is clear that Plato does not believe that he can eliminate homosexual eros, nor all expressions of physical love between men. Indeed, their existence is seen as an indispensable condition for those who will eventually be borne aloft by their wings. Without eros they would have no reminder of real beauty; without eros their wings would not grow. It is also essential for the ascent that such love is restricted in its physical form. It is not clear what the restrictions involve, but such relationships obviously must not reach the point where they become, as Socrates has described them, the lust of a wolf for a lamb.

The myth of the charioteer and his horses, however, is not relevant solely to those who pursue wisdom. It relates also to those who live a less exalted life in pursuit of honour. Such men in an unguarded moment will be caught unawares by their unruly horses who will constrain them to snatch at what the world regards as the height of felicity and consummate their desire. Such couples will enjoy this pleasure again, but sparingly, because it does not have the consent of their whole mind. They will not attain their wings immediately, but because they have tried to do so and this effort comes also from the madness of love – in Socrates' view a divine madness – they will attain them eventually.[68]

Ultimately, then, it is not only those men who are restrained in the matter of sexual love, but those who are more indulgent in this direction, who gain their wings and real knowledge. It will simply take the latter longer to do so. It is clear, also, that Plato feels genuine compassion for those caught in the agonies of homosexual eros. For all he has despised ungoverned sexual desire, depicted as the shambling, ugly and wicked horse, when this horse is subdued it is to be allowed some enjoyment for all that it has suffered. Sexual anxiety is placated by drawing a distinction between satisfaction and satiation, a distinction which involves more than a simple matter of degree. It is imbued with notions of spirituality as well as restraint.

Even those who cannot fulfil the requirements of the philosophic nature are recipients of Plato's sympathy and understanding. For although they are more abandoned in their love-making, they acknowledge that what they do does not carry the consent of their whole minds. They too eventually win their wings.

But however long it may take individual souls to regain their wings, one things is clear. It is always initiated by erotic love; the erotic is an integral part of the ascent. Intense sexual feeling must be experienced; the physical manifestation of such feelings must be encountered, understood and then left behind as the ascent begins. Plato does not wish to eliminate, but to control such feelings in men. He wishes only to eliminate the kind of erotic feelings and love-making between men which, in gross and abandoned form, might be seen to simulate the love between men and women that is merely part of the animal reproductive process.

But if the first step on the way to philosophy is restrained homosexual love, and only the love of a man and a boy can stimulate the recollection of eternal beauty, this leaves women no means of making the ascent. The female body and the feminine cannot be part of the process. The feminine, by definition, is that which is left behind when the soul is raised by its wings to the realm of reality.

There is nowhere any suggestion that a similar loving relationship between women, with no prospect of the production of children, paves the way to the same vision of the eternal. There is scarcely a mention of lesbian love in the dialogues, and when reference is made to it in *The Symposium* – in a speech on love by Aristophanes – it is made clear that it is an inferior form of love to that between two men.[69] Neither is there any suggestion that the love of an older woman, past childbearing years, for a boy might admit her to the realm of philosophy.

Hans Kelson has claimed that it cannot be doubted that the eros of Plato is not what would be termed friendship today. Even on the highest spiritual plane it is something which has a most explicit sexual basis. He adds, however, that it is always, exclusively, the love of youth. It can be inferred from this, he says:

> That Plato not only had no comprehension of the sexual peculiarities of women, but that love of women must have been completely foreign to him . . .[70]

However, the power of sexual love between men has to be cleansed of the animal aspects which are associated with the female. Plato's fear of female sexuality is only assuaged by differentiating it in every way, even in its physical expression, from male sexuality. Plato clothes homosexual eros in myths and metaphors from which, in *The Phaedrus*, he excludes any notion of the feminine.

The spiritual side of love-making which causes the growth of the wings of the soul and which carries the soul back to the realm of true love and knowledge applies only to the love of men and boys. It is only from a starting point of physical attraction between man and boy that recollection of the Forms is aroused. Only the sight of a beautiful male body causes the ferment and throbbing which are a reminder of absolute beauty. Only the best souls, before birth, have perceived most of the divine, and consequently have the memory of the eternal. The best souls have fallen into male bodies in their first incarnation.

Plato justifies what he perceives to be the unavoidable and, in its physical sense, somewhat alarming, desire of man for man, by creating for it a metaphysical purpose. The exquisite agony and struggle to attain harmony in love are inextricably linked to the struggle to attain knowledge. In the attainment of that knowledge men's weaknesses are absolved. By understanding and then transcending physical love for each other, men place that love on a different and infinitely higher level than love between men and women.

Women receive no such absolution. Women enjoy sexual union, are unrestrained, and produce offspring. Women must continue to produce flesh from flesh where men can create the spiritual from the physical. Women, trapped in a female body, have no equivalent doorway to that of the male in mutual admiration and celebration of youth through which they can pass to attain knowledge. Women remain caught in immanence and debarred from philosophy.

4 The Immanent Female

The immanent female is the immediate and obvious counterpart to Plato's transcendent male. They are identifiable opposites which take their very definition from their relationship to one another. As such, they represent a fundamental duality in Plato's thought.

The relationship is, of course, that of the superior to the inferior; the one which must dominate and the one which must be held in subjection. Plato believes that while men are capable of transcending physical nature in order to arrive at truth and knowledge, women represent precisely that nature which men must rise above. The feminine necessarily involved the physical, not only in sexual union, but in the entire reproductive process in menstruation, lactation and childbirth. The female, quite simply, can never totally overcome physical nature. Her very existence is determined by it; she is defined in terms of it. Men, on the other hand, can, in certain circumstances, relinquish the physical in favour of the spiritual and, though not at all in the manner of women, can themselves give birth. They give birth, however, to the superior progeny of wisdom and virtue.

For Plato the distinction between male and female, synonymous with good and bad, incorporates a distinction between the spiritual and the physical, between mind or soul and body. Yet again one can look to *The Timaeus* for evidence of the precedence of soul over body in terms of both time and importance. Plato tells us that the only existing thing capable of intelligence must be called soul, and soul is invisible. Fire, water, earth and air are all visible bodies:

> So the lover of intelligence and knowledge is bound first to investigate causes of rational nature, and only then proceed to those that operate through bodies whose motion is derived from others and must be passed on to others.[1]

Soul is once again depicted as a self-moving prime origin from which all else springs. Hence one's first concern in the pursuit of knowledge must be soul.

However, it is important to remember that the dualities which appear in Plato can only exist in relation to one another, and that it is precisely this comparative relationship which gives them definition. Lloyd has argued, quite rightly, that it is this notion of contrast between knowable form and unknowable matter which is at the heart of Plato's theory of knowledge. The distinction she sees as being between mind, the principle which understands the rational, and matter which has no part in knowledge. It is the knowing mind which transcends matter.[2]

What this clearly means is that in Plato's theory of knowledge, which involves an intellectual ascent, only the male, associated with the Cosmic Father, with the Forms, and thereby with clear rational thought, is capable of transcendence.

But it is equally important to remember that the female, associated with Prime Matter, the indeterminate, the formless, the unknowable, is not excluded from the process. She is, in fact, a crucial part of it. What is significant is that femininity plays a part in the negative sense that it represents that which the male must transcend if knowledge is to be attained. Knowledge is only achieved once everything standing in opposition to it, typified by the feminine, has been overcome.

This has particular political significance in relation to the philosophy on which the Ideal State is to be founded and inevitably raises the question of the real status of women the *The Republic*. Plato has made clear that certain women are to be included in the ruling elite, the Guardian Class. But if the female is defined, in the fundamentals of his philosophy, as inevitably and innately inferior to the male, there is an apparent inconsistency which requires explanation.

More than one critic has cited this difficulty in analyzing Plato's political theory. Susan Moller Okin, for example, begins an investigation into women in political thought by pointing out what appears at first sight to be an 'unresolvable enigma' in Plato's ideas about women. She questions how this problem arises in the work of a philosopher who is 'generally consistent'.[3]

Elizabeth Spelman adds further to the speculation concerning the respective role of men and women in the Guardian Class by arguing that Plato's division among parts of the soul, where the rational and spirited parts must control the inferior appetitive elements, is intimately tied to Plato's political views in that his discussion on the parts of the soul and their relation to one another, is integral to his views on the best way the state should be set up. In the state also, the rational part should rule, attended by the spirited part, and both should watch over the appetitive elements.[4]

It is her conclusion that what is learned from Plato about state-hood is similar, therefore, to what is learned about knowledge. If the irrational part of the soul overpowers the rational part, one can't have knowledge. Similarly, in political life, where the rational does not rule, the state will be in utter chaos.[5]

But if one accepts this argument, and it is difficult not to, then the politics of the Ideal State have become really problematic. For if the female is associated by definition with body, and with the appetitive part of the soul, those things which must be relinquished or kept subdued, what exactly is the function of women in the elite Guardian class? They have, by Plato's definition, apparently no right to be there at all. Yet they are there at his insistence and seem-ingly not just because they are needed to breed; indeed, their breeding capacity is to be regimented and minimized to free them for other tasks.

Diana Coole, also acknowledging an apparent inconsistency in Plato, maintains there is a definite dialectic to debates about women's relationship to politics. Western thought, she claims, involves a series of binary oppositions and the male/female opposition is in fact often treated as the primary dualism which is used to illustrate or give meaning to the rest. In political life, she argues, this gives meaning and legitimacy to male domination since it is the male principle which is associated with the superior side of all other oppositions.[6]

But once again, if this argument is accepted, and it is an ex-tremely persuasive argument, then where Plato is concerned, we have come full circle to the same nagging questions. If Plato, who makes precisely these distinctions between male and female, actu-ally believes the basics of his own philosophy, then what of the women of the Guardian class? They are, according to his own theor-etical framework, inescapably inferior. Yet they take full and equal part in the running of the state with the Guardian men. How do they attain this level of equality when they are fundamentally in-ferior, and only superior intellects may govern according to Plato's perception of Justice?

One answer is to say that Plato is what Coole has dubbed 'prima facie' radical. He is one of those thinkers who speak of equality. Scratch this superficial equality, however, and one discovers that women gain equal status only if they jettison all things about them which are perceived to be feminine.

They must, as Coole has argued, subdue not only their feminine characteristics, but their relationship to reproduction.[7] They must conceive as a rare dispassionate act and raise their children as a matter of civic duty.[8]

This is, of course, precisely what happens to women in the Guardian class, though they are not even allowed to raise their own individual children. They are to live, eat and exercise naked with the men. They are to mate only when and with whom they are told, and their children are to be removed from them at birth. In short, it is only at the cost of their femininity and, incidentally, of their traditional sphere of power and influence, the home, that women are afforded an opportunity to participate in public life.

There is a strong distinction here between superficial, or alleged equality, and real equality which would rest, not on the abandonment of all things seen to be feminine, but on a redefinition or a new evaluation of femininity and, consequently, a reappraisal of women's social role.

This is one of the major problems in Plato's political theory as it relates to women, and indeed what is problematic, generally speaking, about 'prima facie radicals'. They do not, in fact, offer equality to woman at all, even when they claim, or appear, to do so. What they do in reality is offer the opportunity to certain women who show a level of ability, a capacity for rational thought, a degree, in fact, of masculinity, to gain the status which should accompany these attributes.

But this does not, in any way, redefine femininity, nor elevate the status of the female in general. Nor does this limited level of opportunity, extended as it is to relatively few women, change the practical, legal or political situation of the majority of women in society. 'Real' women's lives would remain substantially unaltered by the removal from their ranks of the less than feminine – or, in Plato's terms, the more than feminine.

What is certain is that the women of the Guardian class would be very few indeed. The Guardian class in total is clearly a small section of the community, comprising only the most intellectually gifted. Since there was little formal education for women in Plato's day, the chances of there being many who would rise above the strictures and limitations of a very home-centred, domestic upbringing would be very remote indeed. But Guardian women are chosen precisely for their similarity to men. Plato tells us that the law-giver, having picked his Guardians must choose: '. . . women of as nearly similar natural capacities as possible to go with them.'[9] The male sets the standard which women must try to attain in order to achieve Guardian status. The fact that there are to be no private marriages indicates that each Guardian male need not have a female counterpart. The same small group of females might mate with any number of male Guardians. We are told that some men are afforded more opportunities to sleep with women because they are superior Guardians; others are prevented from doing so to stop inferior children being born.[10]

Arguing that few philosophers have been able to break with this pervasive dualism, Coole, however, points to a further, more significant problem associated with the exclusion of female characteristics from public life. It is the fact that such characteristics are not only seen to be distinct from masculine traits which cultivate true knowledge, but that they are also perceive to be threatening. She comments that the earliest writings in political thought seem to be motivated in part by an inordinate fear of the female and a determination to subdue her power at all costs.[11]

This is an extremely important point, one which reinforces the argument that the relationship between opposing terms like male and female, mind and body, is not a purely descriptive one. On the contrary, there is a vital mutual dependence, the one upon the other, in the matter of definition. The notion of male contains within it a necessary distinction from female. Male is not masculine but by the exclusion of femininity.

But the real importance of this is that it is possible for the one to be threatening to the other. The terms male and female incorporate a number of characteristics and these can exist in the human being in varying degree. Masculinity and femininity, then, can impinge upon one another. In so far as women who will be included in the Guardian class are those who can raise themselves to the standards of masculinity, men, alternatively, may be vulnerable to the adverse characteristics of femininity. That they are not totally immune is evidenced by Plato's comment that men can behave on occasion in 'womanish' fashion.

The rigid discipline of all forms of the Guardians' education is indicative of Plato's belief in the potential corruption of even the best souls. In the early stages of their training he tells us the Guardian must be prevent from:

> ... grazing widely as it were in unhealthy pasture, insensibly doing themselves a cumulative psychological damage that is very serious.[12]

The Guardian men are to be protected by every possible means from exposure to unhealthy influence. It must be remembered also that when the women join the ranks of the Guardians they are not simply afforded equal opportunities, they are subjected to the same disciplines. They are removed from association with private families, with their children, with all things which foster and encourage their worst characteristics, the emotionalism and personal ambitions which Plato sees as the inevitable accompaniment to family life.

Plato states explicitly that the greatest good in the state, unanimity, is created by the community of women and children in the Guardian class.[13] What Plato does by his inclusion of women in the ruling elite on terms which mean that they must be more like men than women is to protect his real Guardians, the men, from grazing in unhealthy pasture. They will no longer associate with real women. They will be protected from the unwholesome influence of emotionalism and private feelings with which femininity is automatically associated. By this means Plato believes that he has not only created a method or reproducing the best children but a method of ensuring intellectual and emotional security for the best men.

WOMEN AND PHYSICAL NATURE

The peculiarities of female biology have long been taken to dictate the behaviour and personality of women. And where such behaviour has been deemed to be less rational and less restrained than that of the male, its supposed biological origin has meant that it has been taken to be 'naturally' determined and, therefore, the woman 'naturally' inferior to the man. It is as a result of this that women have frequently been trapped in social situations which reflect what is perceived to be their 'nature'.

De Beauvoir cites the data of biology as the very origin of notions of transcendence and immanence and in addition the origin of male anxiety regarding the female. The egg, she says, is active in its essential feature, the nucleus, but it is superficially passive. Its compact mass is 'sealed up within itself'. She maintains that for the ancient Greeks the form of the sphere represented the circumscribed world, the impenetrable atom:

> Motionless, the egg waits; in contrast the sperm – free, slender, agile – typifies the impatience and restlessness of existence. . . . . The ovule has sometimes been likened to immanence, the sperm to transcendence.[14]

There is, however, an alarming element in the process of fertilization. It is the sperm, representing transcendence, which is consumed by the immanent egg.

De Beauvoir has placed in sharp perspective not only the role of biology in perceptions of male and female behaviour, but the fear factor which is present in the male perception of female nature, a perception underlying political and social consequences.

That the Greeks saw women's behaviour as springing from their biology is evidenced, to some extent, by surviving medical records, though records relating to detailed medical procedures associated with menstruation, childbirth, menopause, are relatively few. Physicians of the period were typically male and concerned themselves more with diseases than natural female functions. The latter fell within the expertise of midwives and wet nurses.[15]

Mary Lefkowitz and Maureen Fant argue that observable phenomena and deduction by analogy rather than human dissection and clinical study formed the premise upon which ancient anatomical theories were based. They comment:

> Hence social norms, such as men's superiority over women, could provide acceptable 'data' about human reproductive systems.[16]

Such 'data', once produced, however, could then in turn perpetuate such norms. An example of this is provided by the fourth century Hippocratic Treatises in which Hippocrates discusses hysteria in virgins and maintains that it is linked to menstruation. The cure, he argues, lies in marriage, sexual intercourse and childbirth.

Hippocrates tells us that many people choke to death as a result of visions, but more women do so than men because the nature of women is less courageous and is weaker. But women's biology is also responsible for the frequency with which they have visions and, as a result, hysteria. He concludes that virgins who do not take a husband at the 'appropriate' time for marriage experience these visions more frequently, especially at the time of their first monthly period, although previously they have had no such bad dreams of this sort.[17]

The explanation Hippocrates offers for this is that after the first period, blood collects in the womb in preparation to flow out. However, when the mouth of the egress is not opening up, and more blood flows into the womb because of its growth and the body's nourishment of it, the excess has no place to flow out. It rushes up to the heart and lungs. When these are filled with blood,

he claims, the heart becomes sluggish and because of the numb-
ness, 'insanity' takes hold of the woman.[18]

Hysteria, or insanity, then, as far as Hippocrates is concerned, is
directly linked with the exclusively female biological characteristic
of menstruation. And this hysteria manifests itself in different ways.
Some girls try to choke themselves, others to drown themselves.
This, says Hippocrates, is because the bad condition of the blood
forces evil upon itself. But the cure is a straightforward matter of
trying to get the blood to flow out in the right direction. There is
an obvious way in which this can be facilitated:

> My prescription is that when virgins experience this trouble, they
> should cohabit with a man as quickly as possible. If they become
> pregnant, they will be cured.[19]

This passage offers, to begin with, an explanation as to why, allegedly, more women than men suffer from visions and hysteria. Such
disorders spring from an excess of bad blood to which women are
clearly more prone because of menstruation. The association for
the Greeks is obvious in the fact that the term hysteria actually
means 'wombiness'. The Greek word *hysterai* translates as 'the latter
parts', a phrase used at the time to refer to the uterus.[20] Woman's
character, therefore, was seen to be influenced by her susceptibil-
ity to diseases causing irrationality and uncontrolled behaviour, and
those diseases are seen to spring from her biological or sexual nature.

More important, however, is that the cure for such problems is
seen to lie not simply in encouraging young women to fulfil their
reproductive role, but in encouraging them to do so as quickly as
possible. This means their being placed at a very early age under
the physical and emotional control of their husbands within the
institution of marriage, and subjected, barely into their teens, to
the responsibilities and strictures of motherhood. It is significant
that Hippocrates speaks of 'virgins who do not take a husband at
the appropriate time', and then goes on to speak of the onset of
their first monthly period. This indicates his belief in the advisabil-
ity of a very early marriage for girls, at least by modern standards.

Such marriages, however, were actually commonplace in classical Athens, the husband generally being much older than his
bride.[21] Xenophon's *Oeconomicus* gives a good example of this. In
his description of the domestic arrangements of the Athenian household the bride in question is fifteen years old, her husband a man
of thirty.

The *Oeconomicus* also provides evidence of the contemporary attitude to female nature in general, evidence which is in many ways consistent with what Hippocrates has to say. The husband, Isomachus, instructs his young wife in her household duties after, he says, she is 'docile' and 'domesticated'.[22] According to Helen King in *Bound to Bleed*, this 'domestication' is like the taming of an animal. She sees the girl's upbringing as being represented as the 'taming' or 'breaking in' of a filly. Marriage is the end of this process: 'marriage also opens the process of submission to the yoke of Aphrodite.'[23]

In other words Isomachus' mention of his wife's docility is a reference to the fact that she has, before receiving her husband's instruction, lost her virginity to him. This has been a necessary first stage in the process of her education. It is a reference which reflects Hippocrates' contention that young virgins are liable to hysteria and that the cure is provided by their having sexual intercourse.

Isomachus' wife, though she shows no sign of hysteria and is, in fact, described as having a 'masculine mind', must nevertheless be prepared in the appropriate way for instruction.[24] This essential preliminary is due to the fact that she is, after all, however rational she may seem, merely female, and the potential for hysteria resides in all women. Sexual intercourse and male domination are therefore seen to be a preventive as well as a curative activity.

This particular bride is receiving her initiation to marriage and instruction in household duties at roughly the 'appropriate time' in Hippocrates' terms. She is not much past puberty and has left the control of her father's house for that of her husband, and lost her virginity, just at the point where the unfortunate symptoms of hysteria might emerge were they not prevented from doing so. She has made the transition from childhood to sexual maturity without the emergence of this problem and her potentially irrational nature has thereby been kept in firm control.

Commenting on the Hippocratic Treatises, Lefkowitz argues that the doctor proceeds on the assumption that the causes of mental disorders in young females are sexual in origin. The cure for the problem of hysteria being a means of getting the blood which is causing the problem to flow in the right direction, Hippocrates prescribes, not a surgical procedure such as hymenectomy, but social conformity, marriage and pregnancy.[25]

Alternatives might exist, but the most attractive proposition is seen to be that which reinforces the social norm. The simplest answer is one which not only takes care of the medical problem but, at the same time, places the potentially anti-social female under the control of the more rational and altogether superior male.

However, the physical problems of women, related to their biological structure, were not confined to young virgins and certain problems might continue, still others emerge, after marriage. All women might be subject to all manner of problems related to the womb. In other Hippocratic Treatises the womb is said to wander throughout the body.[26] A womb that has lodged near a woman's head causes torpor and foaming at the mouth. A womb that has moved towards the hips causes a loss of menstruation. A womb that has moved towards the liver, a problem said to affect old maids and widows in particular, causes loss of voice, teeth chattering and darkening of colour. As a remedy for this the doctor must push his hand down below the patient's liver, tie a bandage below her ribs, open her mouth and pour in very sweet-scented wine, put applications on her nostrils and burn foul-scented vapours below her womb.[27]

Bizarre as these remedies might seem today, their significance is more than medical and cannot be attributed to mere ignorance of female anatomy. The cure in all cases lies in the hands of the male, be it husband or doctor, who is seen thereby to control the potentially uncontrollable. Once again one can see the political and social consequences. What is perceived to be the female's 'natural' condition is used to justify her legal and social situation.

Such notions, it can be argued, lie deep within Greek culture. Lefkowitz, for example, maintains that descriptions of the womb in its wanderings and the remedy applied by the doctor can be likened to the behaviour of the insane women of Greek myth, where the remedy for their insanity invariably involved some sort of male intervention. She points out that a male prophet's intervention is needed to restore the sanity of the wandering daughters of Proteus. Io, wandering pregnant, with horns like a cow, is restored to her normal form and delivered of her child by a touch of Zeus:

> Male attention, therapeutic or punitive, is needed to restore the insane woman to society, or the dislocated womb to its normal function.[28]

According to Plato, male intervention is also needed for the creation of woman in the first place. The notion of the wandering womb appears in *The Timaeus* by way of explanation of the female sex in general. This explanation follows on from Plato's contention that men of the first generation who led cowardly or immoral lives would be turned into women at second birth. It is at this point of time that sexual love comes into being. Significantly, sexual desire of any kind, in the male as well as the female, is characterized by its irrationality. Plato tells us that a man's genitals are naturally disobedient and self-willed, like a creature that will not listen to reason, and will do anything in their mad lust for possession:

> Much the same is true of the matrix or womb, which is a living creature within them which longs to bear children. And if it is left unfertilized long beyond the normal time, it causes extreme unrest, strays about the body, blocks the channels of the breath and causes in consequence acute distress and disorders of all kinds.[29]

This goes on, he says, until the woman's longing and the man's desire meet and pick the fruit from the tree and sow the ploughland of the womb with seeds which will eventually grow into complete living creatures. Plato adds: 'This is how women and the female sex generally came into being.'[30]

This clearly indicates that it is male activity which creates woman and begins the process of reproduction. While Plato attributes irrational desire and longing to both male and female, and describes sexual union as a meeting of the two, it is nevertheless the male which 'sows' the seed in the 'ploughland of the womb'. The male is active, the female passive.

And while Plato states that male genitals do not respond to reason, he also speaks of their lust for possession. The real separation of the sexes takes place when those who long to possess do, in fact, take possession of those who long to submit and bear children. Once again it is male intervention which ends the wandering of the womb. Plato's postscript that this is how women and the female sex in general are created further emphasizes the dominant masculine role.

But, as de Beauvoir has argued, the passive action of the female role in reproduction is at the same time both magical and alarming. It is the male sperm which is consumed by the female egg. It is women who are, thereafter, predominant in the matter of reproduction. It is women who, in the end, labour and produce live babies from their own bodies.

In discussing the origins of western misogyny, Coole also acknowledges this anxiety. She comments that if one examines the male/

female conflict in drama and myth, the female's power emanates from her ability to create new life, and this must be 'defused' if male sovereignty and the rationality associated with it are to be ensured.[31]

The solution to the problem was to accord the male the more significant role than the female in the process of reproduction. She cites *The Oresteia* where Orestes, who has murdered his mother, Clytemnestra, is charged with the crime and defended by Apollo.[32] Apollo's defence of Orestes consists in the argument that it is the father, not the mother, who is the real parent. The mother, he maintains, is not the real begetter, but simply the nurse to the newly sown conception. The begetter is male and the mother is the stranger who merely preserves the offspring.

Coole argues that this notion that the male plays the more important role in reproduction persists throughout Greek thought. She points out that it appears in *The Symposium*, though in slightly different form. In *The Symposium* spiritual love, of which only men are capable, is not only praised as superior to carnal pleasure, but its outcome is also claimed to be a superior progeny.[33]

The passage in *The Symposium* to which Coole refers is that in which Diotima, the priestess, comments that men whose creative instinct is physical have recourse to women and produce children. Those whose creative instinct is of the soul produce wisdom and virtue in general.[34] This is infinitely superior to the production of children who are merely mortal. Wisdom and virtue are immortal, and the spiritual procreation of which men are capable is therefore a superior form of procreation.

It must be remembered also that the magical, passive reproduction of which woman alone is capable, is possible in the first place only by the intervention of the dominant, superior male which, according to *The Timaeus*, constitutes the life force. But this act of siring children is a mere physical copy of real procreation which is completely masculine, entirely free of female involvement, and which is spiritual and immortal. Spiritual reproduction belongs in the realm of the Forms; physical birth resides on earth. Women's frightening physical nature is controlled, therefore, by subjection to the male in earthly love and physical reproduction, and by their total exclusion from the ascent to real love and knowledge.

Plato's philosophical hijacking of the reproductive process has been interpreted by some as evidence of an appreciation, rather than an outright fear, of this mysterious, and exclusively female, function. For example, in *Sowing the Body* Page DuBois attempts to argue that Plato, in fact, rejected a view of sexual identity which rested on contradictions. Plato, she says, has seemed to some to have a fantasy of an exclusively male world. Plato is deemed to regard philosophy as a masculine endeavour. It is pointed out that with the exception of indirect appearances by Aspasia and Diotima, women, whose wombs wander and who are dominated by the unphilosophical parts of their souls, do not appear in the dialogues.

Further evidence of this ideal and masculine world is cited in the *The Phaedrus*, where seduction is an issue between man and man, philosophy and the approach toward the good are the business of male lovers, and reproduction is ascribed exclusively to men who will inseminate each other with philosophy as a sexual act in which women have no place.[35]

But DuBois argues that while one can read into this a phallocentric Plato who had a vision of homoerotics based on the absolute rejection of women from intercourse with men and based on a philosophy that exiles women, one can also identify countercurrents.[36]

She maintains that there is an undercurrent of dialectical movement between the sexes in *The Phaedrus*. There is, she says, a recognition that a definition of sexual identity in terms of contradictories is not satisfactory. Plato, she argues, employs the 'fluid boundary between the sexes' with great seductive power:

> And he appropriates traditional metaphors – the description of the female as defined by inner potentiality, by reproductive interiority – to the person of the male philosopher.[37]

DuBois believes that Plato uses the tension between the sexes in Greek culture to assert the authority of the male in terms of philosophy, but that he also appropriates the female powers of reproduction to the male philosopher.

But while she is right to say that this, of course, indicates an acknowledgement of female power, it need not, and does not, accord any greater status to femininity in intellectual terms. Nor does it eliminate definitions of sexual identity based on contradictories as DuBois has claimed.

DuBois does not actually specify how and where Plato employs 'fluid boundaries' nor what constitutes the 'undertext' to which she has referred. Her argument, on closer inspection, is rather more of an impression based on Plato's use of sexual metaphor, an impression which is not borne out by critical examination of *The Phaedrus*.

The Phaedrus, essentially about love, is notable for its almost total exclusion of any consideration of the female sex. An implicit reference to the female – Plato's contention that those who are sexually abandoned are eager to mate and beget children, like beasts – does not deny contradiction, but to the contrary, highlights it. It draws a vivid distinction between the love of men for boys and the love of men for women.[38]

Plato does not so much 'appropriate' as usurp female reproductive power and, what is more, he also transforms it. Reproduction in the female, however magical and powerful it may seem, is still a purely physical function. Reproduction in the male constitutes the birth of knowledge which resides on a spiritual plane. The mind/body distinction remains intact, and it remains a reflection of the notions of male and female as opposites. Contradiction, separation and distinction, far from being eliminated, are at the very heart of *The Phaedrus*.

The type of power which the female possesses is a lowly version of power which, in its complete form, is masculine. It is not the fact of reproduction but the idea of reproduction which Plato absorbs into his masculine philosophy. The male must first overcome, or dominate, the female in order to establish its masculinity, and then it must transcend any physical connection which is in any way reminiscent of the male/female association. For *The Phaedrus* also makes clear that ultimately even homosexual relationships must be transcended, at least in their physical expression, because this is something base. It replicates physical love between men and women, the end of which is physical reproduction.[39]

The reproductive power of women is also relegated to inferior status in *The Symposium* where Diotima makes clear that this is because it is a purely physical function.[40] Here once again the notion of procreation is not only usurped by men but also transformed into a spiritual, abstract, and altogether superior type of procreation – the production of wisdom and virtue.[41] The mind/body, male/female opposition remains intact, as does the male need to free itself from inferior and dangerous physical association. If Plato cannot, in fact, create an entirely masculine world, he can, and does, create a masculine philosophy.

THE PHILOSOPHER AND THE MIND/BODY DISTINCTION

If one accepts, however, that clear distinctions between mind and body exist in Plato's philosophy and that such distinctions are identified with the male and female, one needs to question again what exactly is the role of women in Plato's philosophy. What are we to make of the apparently contradictory remarks that he makes about women? How are we to interpret his real intentions concerning female involvement in the Ideal State? If Plato's philosophy is founded on the very notion of female inferiority, then *The Republic* seems more of a satire than a work of philosophy as some critics have tried to argue. But most interpretations take Plato seriously on the subject of women. And if one is right to do so then the position of women in the Guardian class is clearly more of a smokescreen than a joke. If this is the case then what is it that Plato intends to hide from us, or to protect in the basics of his political theory?

Spelman, acknowledging the difficulty, describes Plato as having a case of 'psychophilic somatophobia'. She maintains that as a psychophile who sometimes spoke as if the souls of women were not in any important way different from the souls of men, he had some remarkably nonsexist things to say about women. As a somatophobe who often referred to women as exemplifying states of being and forms of living most removed from the philosophic ideal, he left the dialogues 'awash with misogynistic remarks.'[42]

She cites as examples *The Republic*, *The Meno* and *The Laws*. In *The Republic*, Plato maintains that there is no administrative task that belongs to man as man or woman as woman and that natural capacities are distributed in both sexes. In *The Meno* he says that virtue is the same whether it appears in the life of a child or an old man, a man or a woman.[43] On the other hand, in *The Laws* he makes clear that to have more concern for your body than your soul is to act just like a woman.[44] In this dialogue Plato considers that the best penalty for a soldier who has escaped injury by surrender is that he be changed from a man to a woman as the most appropriate punishment for throwing away his shield.[45] Since this is not physically possible the nearest approximation to such a penalty is that the soldier in question should spend the rest of his days in utter safety, and thereby in disgrace. He is a natural coward, and must avoid the risks that only real men can run.[46] The natural

coward, in other words, behaves like a woman and should be condemned to the life of a woman – a life of disgrace.

Spelman poses the question as to what we are to make of this
'double message' about women. On the one hand Plato appears to
affirm the equality of men and women, while on the other the dialogues are riddled with misogynistic remarks.[47]

But what Spelman sees as contradiction may be interpreted in
another way. She examines the passage in *The Republic* which deals
with 'natural capacities' of men and women and interprets it as
meaning that Plato was arguing for a sameness of the souls of men
and women. Nature and soul, however, are not one and the same.
Nature is a term which Plato uses very broadly and can be seen at
different times to mean different things. It may involve ability or
expertise as it does when he allots similar tasks to similar natures
as in *The Republic*, or it may mean something more akin to personality as when he describes the emotional, uncontrolled aspects
of female behaviour.

In designating certain tasks to certain people Plato acknowledges
that women have abilities which may be utilized in the service of
the state. They may have abilities which are similar, in some cases,
to those of men. But the 'misogynistic' remarks to which Spelman
refers indicate his belief in a fundamental inferiority of women at
the level of soul, in spite of any talents they may possess.

In *The Laws* Plato tells us that there is a natural hierarchy of
superiority which should be observed:

> Now the 'superiors' of bad men are the good, and of the young
> their elders (usually) – which means parents are the superior of
> their offspring, men are (of course) the superiors of women and
> children, and rulers of their subjects.[48]

Women, then, stand in relation to men as the bad to the good, the
child to the parent. They are the natural inferiors in society. Ability or talent apparently does not alter this.

Plato's comments regarding virtue in *The Meno* can likewise bear
different interpretations. That virtue is the same in a man or a
woman, does not necessarily indicate that the souls of men and
women are the same. Spelman, while implying that Plato means
just such a similarity, nevertheless acknowledges that virtue is a
Form, and like any other Form, is thereby eternal and unchanging.
Virtue, then, must be the same thing whether it appears in a man
or a woman. But what this means is that it is the Form which is

ever the same, not men and women. Virtue may appear in greater or lesser degree, or with greater or lesser frequency in different human beings. Women might have a certain capacity for virtue which will always be the same quality as in a man, but men may always have the greater capacity. Spelman overlooks a passage in *The Laws* where Plato is explicit about this.

Arguing that the female sex needs to be controlled in the interests of the security of the state, Plato tells us:

> You see, leaving women to do what they like is not just to lose half the battle (as it may seem): a woman's natural potential for virtue is inferior to a man's, so she's proportionately a greater danger, perhaps even twice as much.[49]

This is a revealing passage incorporating as it does a notion once again of what is 'natural' – women are 'naturally' less virtuous than men – and a notion of the dangers of female nature. Failure to keep this under control means running the risk, not just of losing half the battle, but of losing the war entirely. Women may be twice as dangerous as men if left to pursue their own nature, lacking as it is in virtue in sufficient quantity. Plato is not so contradictory as he first appears in his assessment of female worth.

Spelman maintains that Plato insists over and over again that our souls are the most important part of us. Our bodies, she says, are not essential to our identity, they are incidental appendages. In their most malignant aspect, they are obstacles to the smooth functioning of our souls.[50]

She concludes that from Plato's point of view if the only difference between women and men is that they have different bodies, and if bodies are merely incidental attachments to what constitutes one's real identity, then there is no important difference between men and women.[51]

But this ignores the evidence of *The Timaeus* as regards the significance of the placing of defective souls in female bodies to start with. Spelman acknowledges this part of *The Timaeus* but regards it merely as another example of Plato's misogyny. But the whole point of the distinction is that the best souls must be housed in a body which is the reflection of their superiority. Female bodies incorporate inferior souls precisely because of their corresponding inferiority. Were this not so the distribution of souls into male and female bodies might be completely random. There would be no need for it to be otherwise. If the souls of men and women were the same it would be immaterial what sort of a body housed them.

This is further emphasized in *The Phaedrus* where it is the sight of a beautiful male body which stimulates the soul's recollection of absolute beauty, perceived while travelling in the train of the gods. Male beauty on earth is the copy of the Form of beauty in the realm of the divine.[52]

Body, then, is not, as Spelman has argued, 'incidental' to one's identity. It is an integral part of it. While it is soul which takes precedence, which is immortal, and therefore, the most important part of the human being, the nature of the individual soul is evidenced to some extent, at least, by the type of body in which it is placed to start with, to begin its first incarnation as a sexual being. An inferior soul is placed in a body which robs it of its masculine status and thereby of its full intellectual potential.

Spelman's conclusion is that Plato's somatophobia is part of his misogyny. He was both dualist and misogynist and his negative views about women were connected to his negative views about body, insofar as he depicted women's lives as quintessentially body-directed.[53]

This is true as far as it goes. What it overlooks is the fact that the connection between women and body originates in Plato's notion of soul. Women's lives are indeed body-directed. But this is because what women are in the first place constitutes the embodiment of the inferior soul, the soul which, in its first bodily neutral incarnation, has failed to avoid the attractions of physical life and the pleasures of the body. It is as a result of this failure to pursue the spiritual life that the soul is born into a body which befits its character. Should it continue in wrong-doing it will end up in the body of a beast.[54]

Even the best souls may be damaged by their association with body and must struggle with its pleasures and pains in order to escape earthly existence and win their release from the life and death cycle. This notion receives its clearest expression in *The Phaedo*, not least because it contains the personification of the immanent female, afraid of death and bound up in earthly existence, in the form of Xanthippe, the wife of Socrates.[55]

The Phaedo is set in the condemned cell and records Socrates' last hours before his execution. The discussion is on the immortality of the soul but, before embarking upon it, Socrates has Xanthippe removed from the room. Phaedo, describing the scene for Echecrates, makes a somewhat sneering reference to this:

> When we went inside we found Socrates just released from his chains, and Xanthippe – you know her! – sitting by him with a little boy on her knee. As soon as Xanthippe saw us she broke out into the sort of remark you would expect from a woman.[56]

The sort of remark one expects from a woman turns out to be an extremely emotional lament that Socrates is seeing his friends for the last time. Socrates' response to it is to comment that she had better be taken home, and servants lead her away 'crying hysterically'.

The significance of this brief exchange is clear when Socrates begins his discussion by saying that philosophers do not fear death. In fact, they spend their lives looking forward to it and preparing for it.[57] This indicates at once that Xanthippe does not have a philosophical soul. Her distress at the thought of impending death, though it is not her own, speaks for itself.

But the reason why the philosopher does not fear death has to do, once again, with mind/body distinction. The philosopher, Socrates tells us, does not concern himself with the pleasures of the body as much as other men. He does not concern himself too much with food or drink or sexual pleasure. In fact he frees his soul from association with the body, so far as possible, to a greater extent than other men.[58]

The reason the philosopher does this is because the body leads the soul astray. It is a source of contamination which prevents the soul from attaining truth and clear thinking:

> So long as we keep to the body and our soul is contaminated with this imperfection, there is no chance of our ever attaining satisfactorily to our object, which we assert to be Truth.[59]

This is because the body provides innumerable distractions; it fills men with loves and desires and fears and fancies and hinders the quest for reality. It follows from this that real knowledge will only be attainable after death when the soul will be completely separate from and independent of the body.[60]

The attempt to separate soul from body as much as possible in life is seen by Socrates as a 'purification' and it is the occupation of the philosopher. True philosophers, he says, make dying their profession and therefore to them, of all men, death is least alarming.[61]

Body is seen here in its worst aspect, as an obstacle to the smooth functioning of the soul. Those who possess the potential to overcome this obstacle are the philosophers who struggle throughout life to free the soul from its 'unwelcome association' with body.[62]

Now Plato does not explicitly exclude all women from this pursuit. But there can be no doubt that they are symbolically excluded in the person of Xanthippe. Her appearance in *The Phaedo* is in no way merely incidental. Her character is there precisely to draw the distinction between mind and body. Those who are concerned with body fear death, those who minimize their association with body are fearless. Who is it who fears death in Socrates' death cell? Not Socrates, the philosopher, but the philosopher's wife and mother of his child.

Xanthippe's hysteria disqualifies her from any discussion about the immortality of the soul. It is irrelevant to her. Her concern is for the moment, for the immediacy of death and, no doubt, for the consequences to herself in the remainder of her own earthly life. She is, after all, about to be widowed. It is significant that she is depicted with a small child at her knee. Xanthippe's situation is clear; she is inescapably tied to body, to the physical, to reproduction. Consequently, she is led away from the death cell by other women in much the same way that she has been led away from philosophy by the corrupting body. She may not even stay in the same room with Socrates as he prepares to meet his death because she causes a distraction – which Socrates has pointed out is typical of all things associated with body – which impinges upon his frame of mind.

The female, once again, is seen as presenting a threat to the male, in this case a threat to his peaceful end. Socrates does not have Xanthippe removed out of consideration for her distress but concern for his own tranquillity. This is made clear at the end of the dialogue. When Socrates has drunk the hemlock his companions break down in tears. Apollodorus in particular is described as breaking into a 'storm of passionate weeping' which affects everyone in the room with the exception of Socrates himself who comments:

> Really my friends, what a way to behave! Why, that was my main reason for sending away the women, to prevent this sort of disturbance; because I am told one should make one's end in a tranquil frame of mind.[63]

It is women in general who fear death, who are unphilosophical, who are emotional. Socrates' companions are appropriately chastened by the rebuke. Phaedo admits that they all felt ashamed and controlled themselves thereafter. It is clearly a shameful thing for men to behave like women.

At the very last Socrates makes total the exclusion of women from his death cell by taking from them one of their customary domestic functions in the preparation of the body for burial. He insists on taking a bath himself before drinking the poison and while he attributes this act to an unselfish motive, 'rather than give the women the trouble of washing me when I am dead' there is clearly a deeper significance in this final gesture.[64]

Death is the ultimate goal of the philosopher, and Socrates' last act is to cleanse his own body, the body which must be left behind in the pursuit of knowledge, but with which the women would still concern themselves. Socrates takes from the women any involvement with this particular body, the body which may now be dismissed, because it is the soul which is of paramount importance.

Earthly life is of little account, as Socrates reasserts in his last words. He charges Crito to see that the sacrifice of a cock to Asclepius is not forgotten.[65] Asclepius is the god of healing, and sacrifices were made to him either to request a cure, or for a cure effected.[66] Socrates thereby implies that the cure for life is death. Bodily life is a diseased condition of the soul. Death is the release from body and disease and thereby the cure for what ails the soul.

Not all souls can achieve release, however, and those which cannot are those most associated with the pleasure and pains of bodily life. Socrates maintains that this is because a soul which feels keen pleasure or pain cannot help supposing that whatever causes the violent emotion is the plainest and truest reality. A soul which feels this kind of emotion is in bondage to the body because every pleasure or pain has a sort of 'rivet' which fastens it to body, pins it down and makes it corporeal. Such a soul, says Socrates, can never 'get clean away' to the unseen world, but being saturated with body when it sets out, soon falls back into another body: consequently, it is excluded from all fellowship with the pure and uniform and divine.[67]

Women, depicted in *The Phaedo* in the person of Xanthippe, uncontrollably emotional and feeling most keenly life's pleasures and pains, are trapped in the endless cycle of life and death. Their souls do not 'get clean away' to the unseen world of the Forms.

5 The Nature of Women and the World of Politics

It has been argued so far that the female in Plato's thought is innately and essentially inferior to the male, that the female is possessed of an inferior soul and is less capable of rational thought. Women, in Plato's view, are typically concerned with the immediacy of earthly life and with the pleasures and pains of the body rather than the perfection of the mind. In addition, they are not only inferior but threatening, representing as they do the physical, the temptations of the flesh. They are capable of luring men away from the path to wisdom and virtue, and flesh represents all that must be overcome in the pursuit of knowledge.

All this is clearly borne out by the evidence of not one but several of the dialogues. In particular, *The Timaeus*, *The Phaedrus* and *The Symposium* pronounce clear and unequivocal judgement on the female in regard to rational thought. By her very nature she is incapable of such thought, at least in its highest form.

However, one is always lured back to *The Republic* and to the unanswered questions swirling around the female Guardians in a mist of ambiguity. For the threat which women present to men is not confined to the individual ascent to knowledge. It extends also to political life. And this seems, at first sight, to make the female Guardians even more of an enigma.

Plato's Ideal State, founded on Justice, depends upon a notion of universal, rational principles like Goodness, Truth and Knowledge. All political and social arrangements of the state are instituted for the good of the community as a whole and not for any individual or group of individuals within it.

But women's nature, defined in terms of their emotionalism and lack of restraint, expresses itself most frequently in defence of family and, very often, in personal or family ambition. Consequently, women's nature is inconsistent with Plato's notion of politics. It stands, in fact, in direct opposition to the principles upon which the Just State is founded. For women, the private and personal takes precedence over any notion of the public good. The female and the feminine, therefore, are potentially politically subversive.

All this makes women's presence in the Guardian Class seem, at first sight, to be all the more inexplicable. But it must be remembered that the female Guardians are turned, as far as possible, into surrogate men. And it is this which gives us some insight into why they are included in the Guardians at all.

However much the Guardians' sexuality is to be controlled and subdued, they must reproduce. This particular physical function cannot be avoided. It is, indeed, of particular importance given Plato's general belief in hereditary intellect or ability. He stresses that the best parents will produce the best children. Breeding, therefore, cannot be left to choice or chance. Where Plato to eliminate women altogether from the ranks of his Guardians, they would be forced to reproduce in some other way, and any other way would expose them to the dangers of female influence. By mating them with masculine females whose only concession to femaleness in any form is a purely biological function, Plato has avoided this risk.

Women, in some ways in a potentially influential position at the centre of the family, were, in Plato's day, restrained and controlled by the male head of the household, the Kyrios. In the ruling elite they will be controlled in a different way, but they will still be controlled. Women are not so much included as absorbed into the Guardian Class. They are sucked into a masculine world where they will adopt masculine attitudes and values. The entire security of the state depends upon the leadership of an elite group which, to the greatest extent possible, eliminates any trace of femininity.

The communal living of the Guardians, which Plato sees as essential, also means, in effect, the abolition of the female's traditional sphere of power and influence. It means at the same time women's separation, to the maximum extent practically attainable, from their traditional relationship to children, a relationship which constitutes women's more important role in family life. The Guardian women will conceive and give birth; all else will be taken from them.

WOMEN AND FAMILY IN CLASSICAL ATHENS

The social status of Athenian wives, and the extent of their influence even in an indirect sense, has been the subject of much disagreement.[1] It has been maintained on the one hand that women were held not only in seclusion, but largely in contempt. On the other it has been argued that this view has been exaggerated, that it rests on misinterpretation of evidence, and that women, particularly within the family, were both powerful and influential – for good and, sometimes, evil.

Hans Licht, for example, maintains that while the status of Athenian citizens' wives was not an ignoble one, it was nevertheless a secluded, limited and domestic one. Licht adds that the education of girls was strictly limited. A formal education was only spoken of in the case of boys. The most necessary elements of knowledge such as reading, writing and female handiwork like spinning and weaving would be taught to girls by their mothers, and a little instruction in music might be added to this, but nothing was heard of scientific culture. The Greek, says Licht, was penetrated with the conviction that the proper place for girls and women was the women's quarters where there was no need of book learning.[2]

One is tempted to think, however, that if this view were wholly accurate, or if it were a complete picture of the Athenian women's lives, there would be little for the male to fear from female nature or influence. Such repressed women, ill-educated, secluded and completely restricted to the female quarters, cannot really be seen as presenting much of a threat either to their husbands or the state. Possibly for this reason Licht's position has been challenged by more recent scholarship.

That there was a high degree of segregation of the sexes in the Athenian household cannot be doubted. The house was divided into two main areas, the loom room where the women worked, and the Andron, or dining room, where husbands entertained their friends at dinner parties and symposia which wives did not attend.[3]

However, it has been questioned whether this segregation was as total as authors such as Licht have suggested. For example, H.D.F. Kitto has cautioned against the 'fallacy' of assuming that anything for which we have no evidence, such as home life, did not exist.[4] Domestic life, he says, does not appear in Greek literature because Greek literature did not revolve around the individual. It centred on politics.

Kitto adds that certain evidence which does exist can be re-examined and re-interpreted. That wives did not appear at dinner parties is certain, but are we to assume from this that husbands entertained every night and never dined with their wives? If they did dine with their wives, one may question whether they talked of nothing but household management.[5]

Likewise the claim that women were not only segregated but kept in almost total seclusion, virtually prisoners in the home, leading a very retired existence and meeting the opposite sex at religious festivals only, can be challenged.[6]

There is evidence, some of it from the literature of the period, albeit often in passing references, that women did go out of doors, and though they were invariably attended by slaves, this may have been for both propriety and protection, rather than an infringement of their freedom of movement.

A passage from Theophrastus depicts a drunken coarse buffoon, standing by the door of the barber's shop and, on seeing a lady coming, 'will raise his dress and show his privy parts'.[7] There was possibly, then, good reason for not allowing women to go out alone. There is no reason to suppose that indecent exposure, directed at respectable housewives of the time, was any more acceptable than it would be today.

It is also questionable whether the claim that women did not go out apart from attending religious festivals is wholly accurate. Euripides' comment that it is an evil thing to have women coming into the house gossiping at least suggests that women visited their friends, and this would certainly imply some freedom of movement about the city.[8]

Kitto claims also that there is some evidence that women attended the theatre. The ancient *Life of Aeschylus* tells the story of the Chorus of Furies in the *Eumenides* which was allegedly so terrifying that boys in the audience died of fright and women had miscarriages. This is, as Kitto points out, a 'silly enough tale', but its significance lies in the fact that whoever told it obviously believed that women did attend the theatre.[9] This is a reasonable argument. If women never attended the theatre the joke would not have made sense.

The fact that the heroines of Attic drama are frequently strong-willed, even formidable women, has raised doubts about the status and education of the female in Greek society. More than one student of the period has pointed out that Pericles' famous comment on female virtue that, 'Great is their glory who can live up to the nature that Providence has given to women, and hers especially who is least talked of among men, either for good or evil',[10] is not easily reconciled with the fact that Antigone, Alcestis and Hecabe are the heroines of Attic tragedy. They can hardly be described as women who are unknown to men, far less women who are confined and ill-educated.

The notion, therefore, that women's education was confined totally to the domestic and in no way covered the scientific or, indeed, the political – political life being public life-may also be
challenged in the light of literary evidence.

In Aristophanes' play, *The Lysistrata*, the women not only go on
a sex strike to stop the war with Sparta, they also attempt to take
over the running of the city. And while it is true that the suggestion that women might govern the city is intended to be laughable,
The Lysistrata is, after all, a comedy, something equally significant
emerges from the script. Lysistrata gives an explanation as to why
she is able to undertake a public role, ridiculous as this might seem.
The explanation is that she has had an education:

> I am a woman, but I am not brainless: I have my share of native
> wit and more. Both from my father and from other elders in-
> struction I've received.[11]

This passage tells a great deal. In the first place, if women were
totally segregated, one would not expect Lysistrata to have received
instruction from her father, and if they were totally secluded she
would certainly have received no instruction from other elders. In
the second place, though women were not seen as the intellectual
equals of men – Lysistrata herself pleads that she is not brainless
in spite of being female – it would appear that in some instances
at least, it was possible for them to benefit from an education,
albeit an informal education. Thirdly, and bearing in mind that the
playwright here is male, women were clearly not seen as being
completely ignorant and stupid. They may be unpredictable, emotional and dangerous, but not 'brainless', even if a little fun may
be poked at the idea of their having political expertise.

What is more, Lysistrata does not lack confidence or assertive-
ness and is therefore, once again, far removed from the modest,
domestic creature who ought to be unknown to men. When she
discusses the war with Sparta she is asked what business this is of
women. She replies that in the last war the women were too modest to object to anything the men did, but she adds that they did
not approve and they knew everything that was going on. She goes
on to criticize the men for pursuing 'silly policies' and 'mismanag-
ing the city's affairs'.[12]

While this passage reinforces the notion that women were at least
supposed to be a silent section of the community, confined to the
household, it indicates that they might also, by informal means, be

politically aware. The women know at every stage of the war what is going on and have sufficient grasp of public affairs to be critical of the men's conduct of them.

It is true, of course, that fiction, and in particular comedy, need not reflect what actually occurred or could have occurred in the society of the time. There is no reason to suggest that women could have taken over the city or that an Athenian audience would have credited such a thing actually taking place. However, in acknowledging that it is difficult to decide what the evidence of a comic passage proves, K.J. Dover makes the further pertinent point that it is not so difficult to detect usages and attitudes which must be accepted as the background of a joke or comic idea if an audience is to get the point.[13]

In other words, an explanation must be plausible or at least credible, and Aristophanes clearly did not think it was incredible to suggest that women received informal education through their association with their fathers and other elders in the community.

It should be noted too that Lysistrata is successful in her objectives. In the end the men sue for peace both with Sparta and with their wives. The prospect of women in charge of the city may be humorous; it is also alarming – sufficiently so for the men of Athens and of Sparta to stop hostilities and take up the reins of government again in their respective homelands.

In taking over the city's finances Lysistrata also tells us that the women are able to do this because they have been in charge of all household finances for years.[14] Fiction, once again, but supported by Xenophon's *Oeconomicus* which outlines in detail the duties and responsibilities of even a very young bride. We are told that the wife who is a good partner in the household contributes just as much as her husband to its good because the incomings are the result of the husband's exertions but the outgoings are controlled mostly by the wife's dispensations.[15]

But that is not all the wife must do. She must superintend the servants, allotting suitable tasks to each, men as well as women. She must decide how money is to be spent and take care of savings, seeing that they are not all spent at once. She must supervise the spinning and see that clothes are made for those in need. She must look after the corn intake and the making of food, look after servants who are ill, and punish anyone who is a rogue.[16] It can be seen from this that it was no small task to be an Athenian wife.

She was, however, to have her compensations. Isomachus tells his young wife not to fear as she grows older that she will be less honoured, but to feel confident that with advancing years, the better wife and mother she proves, the more will be the honour paid to her in her home.[17]

The situation of the wife in the *Oeconomicus* is, therefore, one of honour, status and responsibility. Though the wife is instructed in everything by her husband – she is, in fact, only fifteen years of age – and she remains under his ultimate control, there is nevertheless the potential as she grows older to enjoy a degree of autonomy in the administration of the household.

This is not to exaggerate the degree of influence that a women might have. Such influence was still severely curtailed and was in the domestic sphere only. It had no bearing on women's formal or legal position within society. Women in classical Athens could not hold public office, own property or conduct legal business. They had always to be the ward of some male.[18] It was the male guardian who gave a woman in marriage and provided her dowry which was returnable if the marriage went wrong.

Should a daughter be unmarried at the time of her father's death she was in no better position. Left as the sole heir to her father's property, she could be claimed in marriage by her nearest male relative, though sometimes men without male heirs adopted a male adult for the purpose of keeping a suitable, legal head of family.

Where this was not done and the closest male heir was already married he was, in certain instances, permitted to divorce his existing wife to marry the heiress. Marriages of this sort took place between half-brothers and sisters, uncles and nieces.[19] This, in fact, happened in Plato's own family. His father, Ariston, having died when Plato was very young, his mother, Perictione, married her maternal uncle Pyrilampes soon after.[20] Such arrangements kept wealth and power within a family, and families were legally and formally male-controlled.

However, what was strictly legal and what was actually done could vary considerably. Informally, women might lead a fuller and less restricted life.[21] How women fared depended very often on where they lived. The laws of Sparta, Crete and Gortyn were all very different from those of Athens. While property ownership usually rested with the Kyrios, the head of the family, there could, in some areas be a Kyria, a female head of family. There is, however, no evidence of this in Athens.[22]

But if Athenian women could not own property, a wife could

manage family finances if the head of family allowed it. While this did not affect their legal position, it meant that some women were able to manage large sums of money.[23] It was also possible for a woman to be appointed 'guardian', and while this had to be with the approval of the head of the family, it meant that the woman could take his place in business affairs.[24]

Clearly, then, there was some recognition that women had abilities and could sometimes undertake tasks usually taken to be the responsibility of the male. This, once again, is not to overstate the amount of freedom, responsibility or influence that women had. But it is clear that their confinement to some extent at least within the home did not necessarily restrict their use of any abilities they possessed where the head of the house allowed them sufficient scope.

These abilities, of course, were still contained within a certain context – that of the private family – and women were always under the formal control of the head of the household. This meant that even where women were allowed a high degree of responsibility they were still exposed, not only to male control, but also to the demands of the personal, to the exclusive bond, created by childbirth, to their own children.

This bond, however, has also prompted speculation in regard to female influence. Philip Slater accords it a very particular significance. Slater argues that the separation manifest in Greek family life gave women a tremendously powerful position. He comments:

> The more the male imprisons the female in the home and takes himself elsewhere, the more overwhelmingly powerful is the female within the home.[25]

Slater offers this as an explanation of Greek homosexuality and misogyny. He argues that the Greek male's 'contempt' for women was not only compatible with, but also indissolubly bound to, an intense fear of them, and an underlying suspicion of male inferiority.

This fear of male inferiority he sees as the origin of customs and rules concerning male/female relationships. For example, he cites the rule that a woman should not be older than her husband, or more educated – incidentally a further indication that women could receive an education of some kind – or be in a position of authority. Such things, he believes, betray an assumption of male inferiority, that the male is not capable of competing with females on an equal basis. He adds:

... the cards must first be stacked, the male given a handicap. Otherwise, it is felt, the male would simply be swallowed up, evaporate, lost his identity altogether.[26]

Slater sees marriage in Athenian society as resembling a relationship between older brother and younger sister, the brother entrusted with his sister's care when he would rather be with his friends, the sister resenting his coldness. He cites the *Oeconomicus* as an example of this and argues that a mother's frustration would be most likely to affect a male child. The wife, resenting her husband's superiority, could punish arrogance, or even masculinity, in her son.[27]

Slater's thesis is an interesting one, though it can be challenged on a number of grounds. For example, it is questionable if the Athenian household was entirely dominated by women as such an argument suggests. The education of the young children was not left solely in the hands of the mother. Specially educated male slaves, 'paidagogoi', were entrusted with the care and instruction of the sons of the household from a very early age and would continue with their education as they grew older.

While little is known about schools, they are certainly known to have existed and a number of professions are recorded. A 'paidotribes' was a physical training master, a 'grammastistes' was a writing master and a 'kitharistes' was a master who gave instruction in the lyre. That they are recorded as being 'masters' indicates that these were typically male occupations, little employment being available to women outside the home.[28]

What this means is that there could have been a strong male presence in the household, even where the father might be absent on public business and boys, at some stage, might have gone to school. One may question also whether, when fathers were at home, they enjoyed no family life and, in particular took no interest in the education and development of their sons and heirs. It seems unlikely. If Lysistrata could boast of receiving her education at her father's hands, and the hands of other elders, how much more likely for a son to receive the benefit of this type of instruction.

Slater's contention that marriage was a relationship which resembled that of brother and sister, the husband and wife resentful of one another, is also doubtful. *The Oeconomicus*, which he uses in support of this, does not really paint such a picture. True, the bride is very young, and is taught everything by her mate but

Isomachus is not depicted as cold and irritable, but, to the contrary, patient and kind. Grube gives a delightfully vivid and, one feels, more accurate description of the couple when he says that while we are presented with a picture against which a modern feminist would rebel, one must remember that the husband is a middle-aged man of some standing, the wife a child of fifteen who has seen nothing of the world:

> .... we should rather be charmed by the delicacy, tenderness and restraint of one who is represented as the perfect Athenian gentleman.[29]

This is not, however, to dismiss entirely Slater's argument. His analysis does point to a strong, if not exclusive or entirely overbearing, female influence in the early lives of the children, boys as well as girls. Parents, as well as nurses and slaves, were known to involve themselves in children's education, and the parent most often on hand would, most likely, be the children's mother.

The notion that female nature was seen by the Athenian male as fearful and threatening comes, in fact, less from the relatively little that is known about home life, than from the way that women are depicted in the literature and drama of the period. While this relies, once again, on evidence taken from fiction, sometimes comedy, the status of which must therefore be carefully assessed, classical drama nevertheless abounds with examples of women who are strong-willed, powerful and aggressive. The authors, however, are exclusively male. What this means is that the depiction of female nature which we receive is a male perception of female psychology.

WOMEN IN CLASSICAL DRAMA

In the light of this it is all the more interesting that not only are the women in classical drama strong, forthright and extremely visible women, they are also women who stand up to men and who, on occasion, challenge the state. Conflict between male and female is a recurring theme in the literature of the period, and what is more, the conflict is often seen, as for example, in Sophocles' *Antigone*, to parallel a conflict between public and private, between personal life and the good of the state.

Women such as Antigone, and indeed in lighter vein, Lysistrata, are seen to step out of their traditional domestic role and into the public arena. They are seen, in other words, to act in an overtly public and therefore political manner.

But what is most important about their behaviour is not simply that it is rebellious, it is the motivation behind it which is more serious and much more alarming. Women do not stand in defence of universal, abstract principles such as justice; they fight in defence of home, family and personal relationships. What this means is that not only are women seen to have a lesser capacity to reason than men, but that they reason in a totally different way by substituting the private for the public, the particular for the universal.

However, the question of how much resemblance these male-defined women bear to the real women of the time has, once again, to be confronted. In her history of women in antiquity, significantly entitled, *Goddesses, Whores, Wives and Slaves*, Sarah Pomeroy challenges scholars who see a direct relationship between the heroines of Greek tragedy and real women.[30] Such scholars, says Pomeroy, argue that the tragic poets found their models among women who were known to them and deduce, therefore, that these women were neither secluded nor repressed.

She acknowledges that if respectable Athenian women were, in fact, secluded and silent, then we must account for the forceful heroines of tragedy and comedy, and question why the theme of strife between men and women pervades classical drama.[31]

Pomeroy's answer to these questions is that the subject matter dictated, to a large extent, what the dramatists wrote. They wrote, she says, of women depicted in epic poetry and consequently could not change their characters. The royal women of epic were powerful, not merely within their own homes, but in an external political sense. To the Athenian audience familiar with the works of Homer, women like Helen or Clytemnestra could not be presented as silent or repressed. Likewise the Theban cycle which depicted the mutual fratricide of the sons of Oedipus; the surviving members of the family were known to be Antigone and Ismene. Sophocles, consequently, could not have presented these sisters as boys.[32]

Pomeroy concludes, in the light of this, that the actions of women in drama did not reflect the lives of real women in classical Athens. However, her argument lacks consistency. For she also questions how dramatists could have become so familiar with feminine psychology if they never had the chance to be with women, and concludes that they would be familiar with their own female relatives and with numerous resident aliens and poor citizen women who did move freely about the city.[33]

This is strangely contradictory. Pomeroy is arguing on the one hand that playwrights depicted women as they did, as strong, politically aware and powerful, because they simply could not change the characters about whom they wrote or the legends in which they appeared, and that these bore no resemblance to real contemporary women. On the other hand she maintains that the nature of women in drama, their passions, emotions, and motivations, are based on the playwrights' perceptions of the nature of the women with whom they were personally familiar.

But it is precisely that nature, and the aggressive, threatening behaviour that it causes, and not merely the identity of the women, which is of importance. It is this aggression and rebellion, born of what is seen to be essentially feminine, which is problematic for men and for the community. The question is not whether women in classical Athens did, or could, challenge the power of the state and commit vengeful and bloody murder in the process. It is fairly clear that they did not; such actions would surely have been recorded. The question is rather whether their nature was perceived in such a way as to point to the dangers of disruption and chaos if such passions were not kept in control. And if women's nature was seen in such a way, it is hardly surprising that they were, indeed, kept in firm control by the men who feared them.

While denying the existence of women like Medea or Antigone among the Athenian matrons of Plato's day, Pomeroy nevertheless argues that there was a fear of the female and, like Slater, believes that it was this fear which led to misogyny. Fear and misogyny spawned the ideology of male superiority but, she says, this was ideology and not fact. It could not be confirmed. Male status, therefore, was not immutable. She adds that myths of matriarchies and Amazon societies showing female dominance were the nightmares of the victors. They feared that some day the vanquished would arise and treat their ex-masters as they themselves had been treated.[34]

Pomeroy herself is implying here that while women did not necessarily act in the manner of a Clytemnestra or an Antigone, the potential for violence and rebellion was thought to be present in all female nature, and consequently it had to be held within the confines of male dominance for safety's sake.

However, it is not simply that women are less restrained, more passionate than men or that they have a lesser capacity for rational thinking which is troublesome. What is more worrying for men is that women have different values, different motivations. When they are depicted as challenging the power of the men, or the power of the state, they are seen to do so because they have a completely different perception of the world.

The context in which Antigone, Clytemnestra or Lysistrata act violently or interfere in political life indicates that women act in defence of their own territory, the private realm, and for the sake of personal relationships. What is significant from the male point of view is that they do not hesitate to do so when such activities come into conflict with the state. What is implicit in this is that women are ever stronger than their customary behaviour and social position would suggest. It is almost as if they are seen to tolerate men and their masculine, political world, so long as these do not impinge upon what is really important. When they do, then the women will do battle. And the overwhelming fear is that they might win.

When Clytemnestra murders her husband, Agamemnon, the *Odyssey* tells us that she brings dishonour on all women. Agamemnon, in the underworld, says of her:

> By the utter wickedness of will she has poured dishonour both on herself and on every woman that lives hereafter, even on those whose deeds are virtuous.[35]

It is another indication that it is the female in general which causes problems. Clytemnestra simply shows us what any female is capable of. Agamemnon himself is guilty of a slaying. The difference is that in his case it has been done by way of a sacrifice to ensure the Greek victory over Troy. Iphigenia, the daughter of Agamemnon and Clytemnestra, is the human sacrifice. Agamemnon chooses victory in war over the life of his daughter.

Arlene Saxonhouse points out that this represents the conflicting values of the male and the female. Agamemnon has been preoccupied with war. According to Clytemnestra's perspective, the perspective of a woman, he deserves the greatest execration for putting war above the interests of the family, for putting masculine pride and vengeance over the sentiments of the family for which he claims to fight.[36]

It is not, however, solely for the murder of her daughter that Clytemnestra takes revenge. It is also for the loss, as she sees it, of her honoured position within the family. Euripides' *Electra* tells us that even though Agamemnon's act was wicked Clytemnestra would not have turned savage nor killed her husband. But, in her own words:

> ... he must bring home with him the mad prophetess; foisted on me a second wife, a fellow-lodger – two kept women in one house.[37]

This tells us something more of the position of the Athenian matron which, according to Xenophon, was one of honour and status. Agamemnon has brought home a mistress and installed her under the same roof as his wife. Her position has been threatened, she has been humiliated. She sees Agamemnon as having a 'second wife', but her own situation reduced to that of 'kept woman'. It is for this, rather than for her grief, that Clytemnestra seeks vengeance. And she does so without regard for the consequences to herself.

A similar theme appears in *Antigone* where, in order to bury her brother, Polyneices, the heroine must defy the decree of Creon, the ruler of the city. Creon has ordered that Polyneices cannot be buried as he is a traitor to the city.

Saxonhouse points out that the tension is once again between the conflicting demands of city and family. The female representative, she argues, becomes masculine in her defence of the family's values in opposition to the masculine interests of the city. Saxonhouse sees Antigone both figuratively and literally stepping outside the bounds of the household in order to protect it:

> Antigone becomes a male warrior similar to those who defend the city as she protects the religion of the family.[38]

Now it is perfectly true that Antigone does indeed step into the male world and challenges its values in support of the family. But Saxonhouse is mistaken in her contention that in doing so she becomes a male warrior. And this is precisely what is problematic about her behaviour and, in the end, why she must die.

The whole point is that Antigone is a *female* warrior, differently motivated and with a different set of values, and is consequently an altogether more frightening prospect. Men challenged by other men know where they stand. The rules of conflict are the same for all and they are honoured by all. Men challenged by women face the unknown, an alien set of standards which they neither respect nor understand.

Antigone cannot be accused of being masculine. If she had any sense of masculine honour she would not act in the way that she does. She would respect the judgement of Creon and the grounds upon which it was made. A woman who displayed masculinity would place the values of the city above those of the family as, indeed, Plato expects his Guardian women to do, even to the point of sacrificing an individual, personal relationship with their own children.

Antigone wishes to bury her brother regardless of her ruler, and in spite of any political point that can be made concerning his honour. She wishes to bury him because that is her task, her responsibility, even her right as a woman.

Mary Lefkowitz points out that strong political women in drama only behave politically in 'closely defined conditions'. Antigone is not trying to avenge or redeem her brother's death, she is seeking only to bury him with the appropriate rites.[39] The difference, she says, might seem trivial to the modern reader but to the Greeks it was essential. Men avenged murders of kin, women prepared bodies for burial and sang laments over the dead. Lefkowitz adds:

> .... Sophocles' audience would have seen Antigone's action as courageous, laudable, but risky (she does end up dead, after all) and certainly within the bounds of acceptable female behaviour.[40]

The problem for men, then, when women act politically, is not the act in itself; it is the grounds upon which it is carried out. It is the type of principle, connected with private life, upon which women make a stand, which is of importance and which is dangerous. It is the type of principle which stands in contrast to those on which the political world is founded.

Aristophanes uses humour rather than tragedy to make the same point in *The Lysistrata*. When the women go on a sex strike in order to stop the war with Sparta, they do so in defence of home and family. Their rebelliousness comes from their frustrations at the deprivations of war. They are tired of their husbands, the fathers of their children, being away for months at a time. Lampito complains that her husband only comes home to put a new strap on his shield and fly off again.[41]

The Lysistrata paints a vivid picture of female nature, one which makes clear once again that women are governed by the physical and as such are rather base creatures. Aristophanes' women are self-indulgent and lustful. They swill wine and make lewd, suggestive remarks.[42]

But in spite of his humorous denigration Aristophanes does not hold women in total contempt, nor does he depict them as ignorant or passive. He suggests that they knew something of politics and that they could be quite well educated. Consequently, released from the normal constraints imposed by the institution of marriage, they are dangerous. As Lysistrata herself comments: 'All our husbands think we're such clever villains', and her companion replies: 'Well, aren't we?'[43]

When Lysistrata is conducting the peace negotiations she is confident enough to tell the men to keep quiet so that the women can clear up the mess they've made.[44]

It is another indication that while women are prepared to tolerate the men's shortcomings up to a point, they will only do so when these do not impinge too heavily upon the harmony of their homes. Where they do the women become fierce opponents, and opponents who can win by creating their own rules of conflict.

There is at least as much caution as humour in Aristophanes' depiction of women, out of control, out of their homes, and running the city. The *Lysistrata*, albeit a comedy, is also a peace play, and it was Aristophanes' plea for the war with Sparta to end to depict the city in the kind of chaos which would ensue if the men neglected their political obligations at home. He presents, therefore, the city in the hands of ridiculous rulers – wine-swilling lascivious women, but strong and successful women nevertheless. It is prudent for the men to give in, in order to regain control. Women, united in their common objective, are capable of victory.

Aristophanes' *Assemblywomen* pursues a similar theme. The women, disguised in their husbands' clothes infiltrate the Assembly and seize the reins of government. Chaos is the result, however, when the women, uncontrolled in their sexual appetites, pass sex laws compelling the young men of the city to sleep with older women before they can have a young woman of their choice. An attempt to implement the law ends in uproar with three old hags quarrelling over one young man who is dragged off-stage lamenting and protesting his fate.[45] Hilarious as this episode is intended to be, it is Aristophanes' caution that the correct solution to the problems of war must be found before any dangerous options are attempted and the city, abandoned and at the mercy of the women, is destroyed.

Saxonhouse comments that Aristophanes in his comedies generally used the female as the representative of the private and the opponent of the public. When the female comes to dominate the city, it dissipates into a realm of sensual satisfaction. She points to the importance of the question of the female in the Athenians' portrait of themselves. They could not describe their city without reference to the women of the city. They recognized the female's claim to be a part of human reality:

> ... the female as a concept was not kept indoors as easily as were the women who, most likely, were not allowed to attend the plays in which they were portrayed.[46]

This is precisely the dilemma which faces Plato in attempting to construct the Ideal State. He must take account of the concept of the female, and cope with female nature into the bargain. But this very nature stands in direct contrast to the notion of the community founded on justice and the good.

When women act politically, they do so in support of children and home, and Plato believes that they will continue to do so as long as home and family continue to exist. It is for this reason they will cease to exist in the Guardian Class. To eliminate, as far as possible, the female principle from *The Republic*, he must eliminate all things which define it and give it validity. It is not just the physical form of family which must be removed but also the idea of family. Women, therefore, must learn or be educated to think like men. Men, for their part, must not be seduced by the personal and the private.

PLATO, FAMILY AND REPRODUCTION

Two sets of problems face Plato in setting up an elite ruling class which includes women. The first is the problem of divorcing women from their traditional sphere of activity, from the family, which is a threat to the very principle upon which the ideal state is founded. The second and more difficult problem is to find a way of radically changing women's unique relationship to the process of childbirth, a central function of family life.

Reproduction must, of course, still take place within the Guardian Class. This is, in fact, one of the main reasons why women must be included in that class in the first place. But the bearing and rearing of children must not continue in the traditional way which is inescapably linked to other aspects of family life. Plato must not only separate the Guardians from family life, he must defend them against it.

This distinction but inter-relationship between public and private, the personal and political life, once again conjures up the notion that while Greek thought is imbued with basic dualities, these contrasts are, at the same time, dependent upon one another for their definition and identity. The public sphere of politics, culture and rational thought, and the private sphere of family, nature and reproduction, may stand in direct opposition to one another, but each is characterized by that very distinction.

Jean Bethke Elshtain has argued that the Greek *polis* was actually a result of a distinction between nature, *physis* and culture, *nomos* in Greek thought. The Greek division and classification of cultural phenomena, she says, was the *polis*, the concept and reality of a structured body politic set off in contrast to the *oikos*, or private household.[47]

She also argues that there was an interdependence of the public and private realm. The private was the realm of necessity, of production and reproduction:

> The public world of politics and free citizenry was conceptually and structurally parasitic upon the world of necessity.[48]

But for all their interdependence the public and the private are seen to challenge one another. Inasmuch as the masculine and feminine can impinge upon each other, so also does the space in which they exist. The public sphere of culture, reason and politics remains superior to the private sphere of necessity and physical reproduction only insofar as it keeps the values of that sphere in subordination to rational male thought.

The political world, in other words, must not only be seen to be separate from the private world; the private world must be relegated, socially and intellectually, to inferior status. The principles upon which family life rests must not be allowed to infiltrate the superior, non-personal characteristics of the world of politics.

Elshtain argues similarly that politics is an 'elaborate defence' against the lure of the familial, with its evocations of female power.[49] Defence, she maintains, implies a set of ideas that must be fended off in order to deal with perceived threats and dangers. She adds:

> At which point such defense becomes a destructive falsification and distortion of reality rather than, importantly, a constructive

way to deal with inner and outer realities will always be a matter for theoretical and moral debate.[50]

This harks back to the very heart of the gender debate and the question of the possible 'maleness' of philosophy and its significance. As Grimshaw has pointed out, even where it can be argued that there are characteristically female qualities, priorities or concerns, the problem always arises of how to conceptualize or describe them. She believes that polarizations such as emotion/reason, concrete/abstract, universal/particular, used to describe differences between men and women, are not only conceptually questionable, but serve to justify the view that the male constitutes 'true humanness' more than the female.[51] Elshtain is making a similar point – that it is a distortion of reality to conceptualize women's concerns in this way.

Nevertheless, such views have given rise to the distinction between public and private which leads to a defence by, and of, the public against what are seen to be, not only inferior but dangerous feminine points of view.

Plato's problem is that the Guardian Class, and ultimately the Ideal State itself, must be protected from dubious principles, which principles women will defend and for which they might, on occasion, step into the public arena, even at the risk of their own lives. The ruling elite must be defended, not simply from the particularity of the family, but from the idea of family and, indeed, the idea of particularity. Such notions, characteristic of the female, are at best irrelevant to rational thought; at worst, given free expression, they might destroy it.

Plato makes clear that the young Guardians' initial education is to be strictly censored precisely to prevent their being contaminated with the wrong ideas. Socrates tells us they must not graze in 'unhealthy pasture', doing themselves psychological damage, but must, instead, live in a healthy climate where all the works of art they see and hear will influence them for the good.[52] But, as Elshtain has pointed out, the public world is necessarily linked to the private world of the family. The world of politics is parasitic upon the world of necessity, reproduction and production. It follows, therefore, that a complete separation of the two will not be easy.

At one level the problem can be solved. Necessary production will be taken care of by one section of the community, the third class in society, the farmers, carpenters and craftsmen. They will provide the material things which are needed by everyone, for the entire community. The Guardians are not to have any possessions of their own. Within that class all things will be held in common and the only reward is that the Guardians and their children will be maintained and have all their basic needs supplied at public cost. They will be held in honour by their fellow citizens while they live, and given a worthy burial when they die.[53]

The problem of reproduction, however, is more acute. This involves not simply commodities but children, the product of sexual union between men and women, and often the focus of emotional and possessive behaviour, particularly in women.

Reproduction is also problematic in two further ways. The first has already been mentioned. It is that reproduction cannot be eliminated from the Guardian class. In spite of the fact that it involves sexuality and the female, the Guardians must procreate because Plato believes that the best of them will produce the best children to perpetuate the class. Though Plato allows that third class parents might produce an exceptionally gifted child, he does not really think that this will happen very often. To prevent the Guardians breeding, therefore, would be to risk ending the line of talented rulers, and would spell destruction for the Ideal State.

The second problem associated with reproduction is that women's unique role in the process is thereby a source of female power. Women give birth and therefore know for certain that they are mothers. Men are only accorded this certainty of parenthood by virtue of the fidelity of their wives and the restrictions of the institutions of marriage and family – precisely those things which will be abolished in the Guardian class.

The first of these problems springs from the fact that Plato did not subscribe to the belief of some of his contemporaries that the female simply nourished and carried the unborn child and contributed nothing to the child's nature. Aristotle, for example, held that male semen was of primary generative importance and what he termed female semen, menstrual fluid, simply provided nourishment for the embryo. He argued that menstrual fluid was like semen, though not in 'pure concoction'. It still needed to be 'acted upon' by pure male semen.[54]

Had Plato believed likewise his problem would have been solved. The Guardians might have mated with women outside their own class, at restricted times only, and produced the necessary crop of children without family involvement. But while Plato indicates in

The Timaeus that he believes that the active and dominant role in reproduction is that of the father, he also makes clear in *The Republic* that the role of the mother is not insignificant to the future character of the unborn child. This is told to us by Socrates in the form of the 'magnificent myth', or, as it is sometimes described, the 'noble lie'.

Socrates holds that the people of the new state must be told this myth at the outset in order to make them accept its social and political arrangements. The myth tells them that they have been fashioned by the gods with metal in their soul. The best have gold or silver and the rest have base metals like iron and bronze. This is a lie for the purpose of forestalling discontent or even open rebellion, and Socrates confesses that it is a 'convenient story'.[55]

Its real significance, however, is that it is used to institute and justify the breeding arrangements for the Guardians. It is here that Socrates argues that the best children, those with silver and gold in the soul, will most often be born to silver and gold parents. In speaking of 'parents' in the plural he thereby includes mothers as well as fathers in the production of the best children.

While he admits that this is not completely foolproof and makes provision for upward and downward mobility of children where the system fails, he is confident that it will most often be the case. It is for this reason that the best female as well as the best male Guardians must be used in the correct way at mating festivals. The best and the best must be mated together as often as possible, inferior and inferior as seldom as possible.[56]

It is obvious from this that if random breeding produced as many gold children as Plato's system of eugenics, there would have been no need for the Guardians to mate at all. It is also obvious that if only the fathers were responsible for the child's abilities and character, there would have been other alternatives. For example, a special class of hetairas, the more sophisticated prostitutes in Greek society, could have been used to cater for the production of the next Guardian generation, without being Guardians themselves. But this is not even considered. The best mothers as well as the best fathers are needed.

The political significance of this is, of course, that whatever his feelings about the female in general, Plato cannot have an exclusively male ruling elite. While women may always be the inferiors of men, some are superior, intellectually speaking, to other women. These cannot be eliminated from the Guardian Class if it is to survive in the form which Plato envisages and, indeed, sees as necessary for the state.

Plato must ensure the purity of what he himself calls his Guardian 'herd'.[57] He must, at the same time, however, defend the herd against ideas which have no part in the world of politics. Consequently, it is women's lives which will undergo the most radical change in the interests of the stability of the state.

Not only will the Guardians come together for the purpose of mating at mating festivals only, and by the decree of the rulers, but children born of the festivals will be taken from their mothers at birth to be brought up anonymously in another part of the city. Guardian women will suckle a number of babies for the shortest possible time, care being taken that no mother recognizes her own child.[58] This arrangement solves Plato's second problem related to reproduction, that of female power which springs from the certain knowledge of parenthood.

Women house the unborn child in their own bodies, endure labour and give birth. Women know that they are mothers because there can be no doubt about it. Fathers, to the contrary, can never actually know that they are the true biological parents of their children. It may be that the social order in classical Athens where women's freedom of movement was certainly severely restricted, left little room for doubt in most cases. But this is not the point. Such 'certainty' rests on reasonable assumption or deduction, not on biological fact. It rests also on wives' fidelity and reassurances.

The doubt and anxiety that the ancient Greeks felt in this regard is clearly articulated in *The Odyssey*. When Telemachus is asked if he is the son of Odysseus, his cautious reply is that his mother says he is: 'I myself have no knowledge of it – what man can be sure of his parentage?'[59] When Telemachus uses the word 'parentage' he means, of course, his father, not his mother. He knows who his mother is – it is the subject of proof. He does not *know* who his father is – other than because he has his mother's word on it, and that is a matter of trust and honour, not proof.

In *The Politics of Reproduction*, Mary O'Brien argues that it is maternal labour which confirms for woman the conception that the child is her child. Fathers do not labour and do not have this certainty. Paternity, according to O'Brien, is a unity of thought – specifically the knowledge of the relation between sexuality and childbirth – and action. The action in which, she claims, men commonly annul the alienation of their seed, constitutes an 'appropriation' of the child.[60]

O'Brien sees Plato, a member of the aristocracy, as a defender of aristocratic values which included a commitment to a hereditary principle. He was, therefore, in the difficult position of having to defend class-conscious devotion to a patrilinear elitism which was rendered problematic by the uncertainty of paternity. O'Brien argues that Plato's solution was to extend the uncertainty of paternity to both parents. Motherhood was to be made as uncertain as fatherhood.[61]

This is a valid argument as far as it goes but Plato, in fact, takes things one crucial stage further. He does, indeed, attempt to create individual uncertainty for women as far as he can. He does not, however, leave the matter there, as O'Brien suggests, creating a situation of uncertainty for both parents. He attempts instead to replace individual uncertainty with communal certainty, a step advantageous only to the male.

All children born after a mating festival are to regard all participants of that festival as their parents and all offspring as their brothers and sisters. But the real object in this is to give certainty of paternity to men. Women are already possessed of certainty in their necessary involvement in the process of childbirth. Even the immediate removal of their children does not alter this. A mother still knows she is a mother; she is a mother because she has physically given birth. Even if her child were to die, she would still be a mother. A man's seed, on the other hand, need not have come to fruition, and he has no real way of knowing that it has, even in the case of regulated mating festivals. Where Guardian women will sleep with a number of Guardian men no father, individually, can possibly have certainty.

What Plato does is to take certainty from women to the extent that he can – that is, in its particular sense, since no mother knows specifically which child is hers – and give certainty to men in the only way that he can – that is, in its universal sense. All men are fathers of all children. It is men who gain and women who lose by the mating arrangements of the Guardian class. Women lose something which they have always possessed – their own individual children, albeit they retain maternity which cannot in any circumstances be taken from them. Men gain what they have never had before, certain ownership of children, since ownership is now a political and not a biological matter. In the Guardian class masculinity retains its dominant position.

Plato maintains that the arrangements are made in the interests of unity which will thereby provide stability. It is, however, a unity of masculinity. In the same way that Plato's notion of the soul in a state of perfection, or in Form, is masculine, his notion of politics in ideal form is masculine in nature. The values which the Guardians, men and women alike, must embrace, are masculine values. Plato's attack on the family and its abolition from the Guardian Class are, in fact, an attack on femininity which threatens masculine ideals.

Plato makes this clear when he says that the best ordered state is one in which as many people as possible use the words 'mine' and 'not mine' in the same sense of the same things.[62] This unanimity is to extend to feelings as well as to more tangible possessions. The citizens, he says, must be devoted to a common interest and consequently share each other's feelings of joy and sorrow. The attainment of this community of feelings is attributed to the fact that there will be: '.... community of women and children in the Guardian Class.'[63] It is this which confers the greatest benefits upon the state and Plato goes on to say that there won't any longer be any of the quarrels which are caused by having money or children or family.[64]

Significantly, Plato does not speak of men and women being common to one another. Nor does he say that all children will be common to all parents. He speaks only of the women and children being held in common by the men. And his reference to the quarrels brought about by having children or family at least implies that it is not men who have difficulty in living in harmony with each other. It is only in their association with women, and on the production of their own children, the certainty of which depends upon the wives' faithfulness and sense of honour, that men are made to be quarrelsome. It is women, traditionally at the centre of the family, who must be held in common because they must be held in check.

This is made clearer still by the sanctions which Plato imposes for infringement of the mating regulations. The punishment falls upon the child conceived and produced outwith the strictures of the festival. Such a child, Plato insists, is '... bastard on both civil and religious grounds.'[65] Consequently, it is to be disposed of as a creature that must not be reared.[66]

Now this is, at first sight, rather puzzling. Why should the punishment fall upon the innocent child? It is the parents, after all, who have dishonoured their Guardian status. And while the child is of an individual mating, if both parents are Guardian then, according to Plato's own firmly-held beliefs, it is most likely to have gold in its soul and, in the fullness of time, be a worthy recipient of Guardian status. Plato himself has allowed that where there might occur exceptions to the general rule, such as a gold child being born to bronze parents, that child should be placed in its appropriate situation in society. It must be brought up to be a Guardian. It follows, then, that the bastard child could be taken into the communal creche and observed to see if it possessed the appropriate qualities for Guardianship.

Plato has also decreed that an inferior child born to Guardian parents should be demoted to the third class, so the bastard child, should it not show the correct potential, could be dealt with at a later stage. But no such humane relegation is even contemplated. The bastard is, most emphatically, not to be reared at all.

The explanation for this is in fact quite simple. A child, born outside a mating festival, would be identifiable. It would be an individual with individual parentage. What is more, the individual parent would be the child's mother. Just as there are no guarantees of biological paternity within the mating festivals, there are certainly no such guarantees outside them. A Guardian woman, who might have had a multiplicity of partners in accordance with the rules laid down for her class, might certainly have mated with a number of Guardian men in flouting them. The transgression need not necessarily have involved an exclusive relationship between one female and one male Guardian. But this means that the Guardian mother, as O'Brien has argued, is the only absolutely certain parent. The female Guardian, carrying and giving birth to a child, alone and apart from the rest, outside the stipulated season, personifies traditional motherhood. And the child could never be absorbed into the anonymity of the young of the herd. The very time and circumstances of its birth could not be obscured in such a way.

Plato therefore sees the birth of illegitimate children not simply as an infringement of the rules but as a characteristically female subversion of the political principles of the state. It is a triumph of the particular over the universal, the private over the public, the feminine over the masculine. The only means of turning that triumph into defeat is by the disposal of the bastard children.

O'Brien points out that the recommendations in *The Republic* have led some feminists to the conclusion that Plato was a believer in gender equality. This, she says, is a short-sighted view. The argument that women could be Guardians was born of the intransigence of biological nature. Women were part of a utopian plan dictated to an extent by the dialectics of the reproductive process.[67]

It is important to bear in mind, however, not only that the inclusion of women in the Guardian class does not constitute real equality, but that superficial equality comes at a price. Women become Guardians by the sacrifice of real maternity, sexual identity, family and consequently power. Yet Plato believes that certain women, exceptional women, will pay the price for what he, and they, perceive to be the good of the community.

PLATO AND THE EXCEPTIONAL WOMAN

It is difficult to determine, however, what constitutes an exceptional woman. She is referred to, but not fully described in *The Republic*. We are told that her abilities must be similar to those of the men, but that is all.

What is more, no woman makes a direct appearance in any of the Platonic dialogues. Only three appear indirectly – Xanthippe, the wife of Socrates, appears in *The Phaedo* and typifies the immanent female, the wife and mother, concerned with earthly life and reproduction. Xanthippe's fear of death indicates that she has an inferior soul and is incapable of philosophy. She is banished from her husband's death cell while he discusses the immortality of the soul. She has no place in such a discussion. Her place is at home.

The other two women who are spoken of in the dialogues, however, are very different from Xanthippe. Aspasia, in *The Menexenus*, and Diotima in *The Symposium*, are both depicted as able women, and they are both in the position of instructing Socrates.[68] Clearly, then, they are women of exceptional talent and provide the only evidence as to what the politically active women of the Guardian Class would be like.

The two differ, at first sight, in at least one respect. Aspasia, like many other characters in the dialogues, was based on a real person. No priestess by the name of Diotima is thought to have existed at all. However, on closer inspection, it is questionable whether the Aspasia of *The Menexenus* is a faithful portrayal of the real character. The historical Aspasia, born at Miletus in Asia Minor, was the mistress of the famous Greek orator, Pericles. Her status as a foreigner meant that they could not marry, but they lived together until Pericles' death. Their relationship appears to have been an unusual one for the time, Aspasia gaining fame in her own right as an intellectual. She is mentioned in the works of four of Socrates' pupils – Aeschines, Xenophon, Antisthenes and Plato.[69]

However, certain things said of Aspasia in *The Menexenus*, not least the reference to her involvement in events which took place after the death of the real Aspasia, suggest that the character of the dialogue is more likely to be Plato's creation.

Diotima is introduced in the middle of *The Symposium* and is described simply as a woman from Mantinea. But we are also told that she is accomplished. She is said to have intervened with the gods to avert plague threatening Athens, and has succeeded in postponing it for ten years.[70] Diotima, then, is clearly no ordinary woman; she is a woman to whom the gods listen.

However, as K.J. Dover points out, though Diotima is a genuine Greek woman's name, there is no evidence outside *The Symposium* for a female religious expert of this name. As further evidence of the fictitious nature of Diotima, Dover adds that it would be unlikely that such a person could have existed who taught Socrates a doctrine containing elements which were specifically Platonic and not Socratic.[71]

This anachronism which Dover identifies suggests that Diotima is also a dramatic device for presenting ideas which are Plato's own, and neither those of Socrates nor of a female mystic. This means that the depiction of both women, the real and the fictitious, is a means of expressing the Platonic doctrine.

But this raises a further fascinating question. Why should crucial aspects of Plato's philosophy be expressed by women? Dover questions in particular Plato's motive in putting an exposition of eros into the mouth of Diotima. He suggests that the reason might be that Plato wished to make the praise of paiderastia, which this exposition contains, disinterested.[72]

In other words, if a female offers a vindication of the love of men for boys, this would be more acceptable than the exposition of any man who might be seen to be justifying his own desires and behaviour.

Focussing also on Plato's erotic theory David Halperin likewise questions why Socrates' instructor should be female, and considers that gender here is of some importance. Halperin's argument is that Diotima's femaleness serves to thematise two of the most original elements of Plato's erotic theory. The fact that Diotima is a woman, he says, signals Plato's departure from certain aspects of the sexual ethos of his male contemporaries and enables him to highlight some of the salient features of his own philosophy.

He argues that two mutually conflicting aspects of femaleness are contained in Plato's philosophy. The first is the Greek stereotype of women as less able than men to resist pleasure and temptation. Women are seen to enjoy sex too much and to become insatiable in their sexual appetites. According to the second stereotype, women do not possess a desire that ranges from one object to another, stimulated by such cultural values as beauty and nobility. Instead their desire is dictated by their physical nature which aims at procreation and fulfils itself by 'drawing off substance from men.'[73]

Halperin claims that Plato's conception of male eros is not hierarchical but reciprocal; it is not acquisitive but creative:

> Plato's model of successful erotic desire effectively incorporates, and allocates to men, the positive dimension of each of these two Greek stereotypes of women, producing a new and distinctive paradigm that combines erotic responsiveness with (pro)creative aspiration.[74]

What Halperin is arguing, then, is that Plato's exposition of eros through the mouth of a woman introduces a 'feminine' dimension into his theory of love. Plato incorporates in male eros the male-female reciprocity of sexual pleasure and female procreative ability.

As far as procreation is concerned, Plato certainly 'incorporates' or, as has been argued earlier, 'usurps' female procreative power in his erotic theory. The matter of reciprocity, however, is quite different.

The Symposium does not present a theory of reciprocity in male-male relationships. On the contrary, the relationship between Socrates and Alcibiades emphasizes the problematic nature of relationships between men and youths precisely on the basis of the differing roles they must play. The *erastēs*, the older man, and the *erōmenos*, the young object of his desire, stand in a very specific relation to one another. The *erastēs*, as Dover has pointed out, takes the dominant and active role in sexual encounters with young men. The *erōmenos*, for his part, must yield reluctantly to his lover so as not to be associated with the passive role of the female.[75] Winkler's image of the *kinaidos*, the caricature of the sexually deviant male which, he maintains, was used as a 'scare image' for men, places such encounters in true perspective.[76] There were clearly unwritten rules or codes of behaviour governing the relationship between man and boy and the effeminization of the boy did not, or at least should not, enter into it.

It is precisely this which causes Alcibiades' humiliation in *The Symposium*. He is left in the position of having offered himself to Socrates – and of being rejected into the bargain. Alcibiades makes clear that he has arranged to be alone with Socrates in order that Socrates should attempt physical intercourse with him. But Socrates does not.

Alcibiades tells us that his motive was that in return for his favours he would be able to find out all that Socrates knew.[77] This is another indication that such relationships were supposed to conform to some sort of code. The older man is seen as guide or mentor to the young who pays for his intellectual training with sexual favours. But the older man is supposed to initiate the physical contact.

When Socrates fails to do so, it is left to Alcibiades to speak of love and tell Socrates that he is prepared to comply with his, Socrates', assumed desires. It is submission which Alcibiades offers, and he tells Socrates that the disapproval of wise men, which he would incur if he refused to comply with his wishes, would cause him more shame than the condemnation of the ignorant if he yielded.[78] Alcibiades acknowledges here that he is not supposed to enjoy sexual relations with an older man but may be forgiven for indulging in them in exchange for the knowledge which Socrates can give.

The fact that Alcibiades has offered himself casts obvious doubt upon his reluctance, and it is this, added to his rejection, which causes his humiliation. Socrates, ought, in the correct order of things, to have made the first approach, and Alcibiades has assumed, wrongly as it turns out, that his failure to do so is out of reticence, that Socrates is afraid to speak of his passion.[79]

Socrates, in fact, rejects the younger man on the basis that mental vision is superior to physical vision. He tells him in no uncertain terms that if he hopes to exchange his physical beauty for intellectual gain, then he is hoping to get the better of the bargain. He is trying to exchange 'dross for gold'.[80]

The beauty associated with physical pleasure is, therefore, of no value to Socrates. Real love does not exist at a physical level. Any reciprocity of feeling, then, must exist at a non-physical level, and in this it is wholly unlike the love of man for woman.

This notion is repeated in *The Phaedrus* where the boy sees himself 'reflected' in the eyes of his lover and consequently identifies with his desire and wishes to share his bed. But Plato stipulates that physical love between them must be restricted and restrained.[81] This does not in any way parallel the love between men and women which, as Halperin argues, is seen to be excessive and insatiable in its pursuit of pleasure. It is important to remember too that whatever the extent of physical contact between man and boy – and Plato does not specify how far this should go – it must eventually be transcended altogether in the pursuit of real love. The reciprocity of feeling takes on a spiritual and not a physical significance.

What Halperin sees as Plato's attempt to introduce the feminine into his theory of love is, in fact, an attempt to reject the feminine altogether. The physical pleasure associated with the female must be controlled in men, although in their earthly existence they cannot avoid being exposed to its influence, and then, with the restraint and experience of age, it must be abandoned completely.

Physical love, like physical procreation, is a vulgar version of the Form of love and the birth of knowledge which are attained only by those who can transcend the physical. This does not include women, as Diotima makes clear. It is not only the praise of boy-loving in the correct way but the denigration of femininity and the relegation of normal female functions to inferior status which are expressed by Diotima.

This is true also of Aspasia. The subordination of the feminine to the masculine, the acceptance of the supremacy of masculinity by women, is what both Plato's exceptional women teach. That their opinions are not to be taken lightly is evidenced by the fact that they are both presented as dominant, even aggressive women. Socrates is at least superficially deferential to both. In the case of Aspasia he tells us that he was made to repeat one of her speeches and almost got a flogging if he forgot.[82] In the case of Diotima, he speaks of his admiration for her wisdom and confesses that he has put himself to school with her.[83]

Both women are alike in another respect. Not only are they strong, dominant characters but while both are identifiably female, neither is conspicuously sexual. H.D. Rankin describes Aspasia in particular as 'a rather unsexed Great Mistress'.[84]

This lack of sexuality is, of course, something which Plato would demand of his guardian women. Like guardian men, they must have their appetitive elements in control. Their sexual appetites must be subordinated to reason, their souls kept, as far as possible, in harmony.

A further, and equally significant similarity between the women is that they both diminish the importance of women's childbearing role. Diotima subordinates the birth of live children to the birth of wisdom, the progeny of masculinity.[85] Aspasia attributes real motherhood to the motherhood of country, not woman; it is the country to whom everyone owes first allegiance.[86]

In *The Menexenus* Aspasia speaks of those killed in war, and tells us that they are natives sprung from the soil living and dwelling in their own true fatherland:

> And nurtured also by no stepmother like other folk, but by that mother-country wherein they dwelt, which bore them and reared them and now at their death receives them again to rest in their own abodes.[87]

The earth, then, has not only fed and nurtured the soldiers, it is she who has given them birth and life. Physical parenting by real women is of no account, it seems, and private and personal allegiance cannot come before allegiance to country. That this is expressed by a woman, an exceptional and gifted women who has risen above the intellectual potential of most, perhaps gives the notion a greater credibility than it would otherwise have had.

In much the same way that Dover has argued that Diotima's praise of boy-loving might be seen to be disinterested in the light of her femaleness, so also might Aspasia's dispassionate contention that real motherhood does not belong to flesh and blood women.

It is interesting too that this notion parallels the 'magnificent myth' of *The Republic* in which the people are told that they must think of the land in which they live as their mother, while all fellow citizens are their brothers born of the same mother earth.

Socrates maintains that first the rulers and the soldiers, and then the rest of the community, must be persuaded that the upbringing and education they have received was all in a dream. In reality they were fashioned and reared, and their arms and equipment manufactured, in the depths of the earth, and Earth herself, their mother, brought them up, when they were complete, into the light of day.[88]

The myth, an acknowledged lie, must become a reality for all. The biological and sexual reality of childbirth must be hidden and its significance diminished in favour of the mythical parenthood of God the father, who places gold, silver and bronze in the soul, and Earth the mother, to whom everyone owes allegiance. Personal life, in the form of family, with wife and mother at its centre, rivals the just state. Plato, therefore, eliminates family life for the Guardians and normal motherhood, which cannot be eliminated, is regimented, controlled and stripped of its potential power.

Aspasia's pronouncements serve a similar purpose. They indicate where all citizens' priorities and duties lie. Of first importance is duty to one's country. It is the earth that has given birth to man who, Aspasia tells us, surpasses all other animals in intelligence and alone of animals regards justice and the gods.[89]

Once again a parallel can be seen between this and the foundation of the Ideal State. The Ideal State is the just state governed by those with the highest intellect. It is justice and the gods that dictate how intelligent men behave. According to Aspasia, those who are just and whose intellect perceives the divine can see proof of the supreme motherhood of the land.

Every creature that brings forth, she says, possesses a suitable supply of nourishment for its offspring. This is, in fact, the test of whether a woman is truly a mother or not. It is the fruits of nourishment which bestow motherhood upon her.[90]

It is this which also bestows motherhood upon the land. For the land has likewise produced human nourishment from which the whole race of mankind is richly fed. Aspasia concludes, therefore, that it is the land which is the true mother of this creature called man:

> And proofs such as this one ought to accept more readily on behalf of the country than on behalf of a woman; for it is not the country that imitates the woman in the matter of conception of birth, but the woman the country.[91]

This is yet another instance of the exclusively female functions of childbirth and motherhood being relegated to the inferior status of a second-rate, vulgar version of something which has a finer form, though some have interpreted it rather differently.

Arlene Saxonhouse, for example, sees this passage as increasing the significance of the female role in Plato's politics. She argues that he incorporates a notion of the female in his philosophy in terms of female procreative power.[92] It is a similar argument to that of Halperin, who contends that the notion of procreativity is incorporated in Plato's theory of male eros.

Saxonhouse sees Aspasia's reference to mother earth as reflecting an Athenian myth of autochthony. But she points out that traditionally the autochthony myth excluded the female. Men could be born without benefit of a human mother. The male seed was simply planted in the soil, and women could be left out of the origins of cities. Aspasia's insistence that we recognize the place of the female, Saxonhouse maintains, is an insistence that without the female there would be no political community.[93]

According to this argument Aspasia's use of the autochthony myth and the reference to the earth as 'mother' raise the status of the female and her political significance. Aspasia is therefore seen to educate Socrates in an 'alternative' view of politics that focuses on maternity rather than paternity.

But Saxonhouse, like Halperin, misses the point that in taking over the notion of childbirth as an important aspect of his philosophy, Plato alters it significantly in the process. When Plato 'appropriates' the idea of childbirth and uses sexual metaphor, as in *The Phaedrus* and *The Symposium*, to describe the creation of knowledge, he transforms it at the same time from the animal process associated with the female, to an intellectual process typical of the male. Women provide an inferior, if necessary, version of reproduction. In its finer form, reproduction is masculine. It involves the birth of knowledge which is a product not simply of intellect, but of soul, guided by intellect.

Aspasia's position in *The Menexenus* is much the same. She ousts women from their traditionally significant role in the reproductive process by pointing out that real motherhood belongs to the country. The motherhood of which women are capable is a mere 'imitation'; the country takes precedence. It is the country for which the soldiers in the war have died. The earth, their original womb, received them again in death. Women's role in the political order remains one of necessity, but necessity subordinated to reason. Necessity dictates that women must still provide physical reproduction; reason dictates that real reproduction takes place at an abstract level. While earth is described as 'mother', this motherhood contains no notion of femininity. Plato draws a distinction between woman and mother that allows of this exclusion. Men spring from the soil and, as in the autochthony myth which Saxonhouse cites, there is no female involvement in the process.

Diotima teaches a similar lesson, though once again Saxonhouse interprets it differently by placing a particular significance on Plato's use of the language of reproduction. In *The Symposium* all the guests are required to make a speech about love, and Socrates, recounting a speech taught by Diotima, relies heavily on references to pregnancy and birth. Saxonhouse sees this as associating eros with the creativity of the feminine. In Socrates' speech, she claims, the female is not vulgarly associated with the body as it has been with all the previous speakers.[94] She sees the male in *The Symposium* transformed into the female, since Plato depicts him as being pregnant with ideas.

But this overlooks yet again the significantly altered character of pregnancy and birth. They are no longer feminine, they are masculine. It is not the male who is transformed into the female, but exclusively female, and incidentally extremely potent, functions which are usurped by the male.

Plato makes the corresponding superiority and inferiority of male and female clear at the outset when he gives us Diotima's description of the birth of Aphrodite as being the outcome of an encounter between Contrivance and Poverty. Contrivance is the father, Poverty the mother. Where Aphrodite takes after his mother – and significantly Diotima says 'his' mother, Aphrodite therefore is male- he is poor, hard and weather beaten, shoeless, homeless and lives in want. But because he is also his father's son, he contrives to get for himself what is beautiful and good. He is bold and forward and strenuous, he yearns after knowledge and is a lover of wisdom. When he meets his death he comes to life again through the vigour he inherits from his father.[95]

The dominant role, then, in the procreation of Aphrodite is the masculine role. It is from his father that Aphrodite gains his thirst for knowledge and the impetus to pursue the beautiful and the good.

Diotima tells Socrates that all men have a procreative impulse which is both spiritual and physical. There is something divine about this and, in procreation and bringing to birth, the mortal creature is touched with immortality. But, crucially, there are different kinds of procreation, and Diotima relegates physical procreation, with which women are inevitably associated, to inferior status.

Those whose creative instinct is physical, she says, have recourse to women, and show their love in this way believing that they can secure immortality by begetting children. But she adds:

> there are some whose creative instinct is of the soul, and who long to beget spiritually, not physically, the progeny which it is the nature of the soul to create and bring to birth.[96]

The progeny to which Diotima refers is wisdom and virtue. And this passage clearly indicates that women represent the physical, not the spiritual impulse to procreation.

Men who cannot rise above the physical impulse 'have recourse to women' and produce inferior offspring. Those who would bring spiritual children to birth search for a beautiful partner. It is made clear here, as in *The Phaedrus*, that the beautiful partner is male. Homosexual eros has once again taken over the female's reproductive power, if not her function, and turned it into a superior, abstract version of reproduction which is totally distinct and distinguishable from the baser form.

Diotima emphasizes the qualitative difference, both in the relationship and in the offspring it produces. She maintains that the partnership of those involved in spiritual procreation will be far stronger and the bond of affection will be stronger than between ordinary parents because the children that they will share will surpass human children by being immortal as well as beautiful.[97] Everyone, she says, would prefer such children to children of the flesh. Where men have gained honour, even worship, it has been on account of their spiritual children.[98]

The distinction that Plato draws here between the love of men for women and the love of men for boys, and the corresponding difference which lies in two forms of procreation, places the male and the female in opposition to one another. They are not only distinct but in conflict, those who pursue immortality begin with the love of boys, while those who have recourse to women are lured away from the immortal.

Diotima's contention that the right use of feelings of love for boys ends with the ascent to absolute beauty echoes *The Phaedrus*, in which the sight of a beautiful boy provides the reminder of beauty perceived by the soul before birth.[99] It is also consistent with the notion of the intellectual ascent described in the same dialogue where souls regrow their fallen wings as a result of homosexual eros and rise up again to the realm of the gods.[100]

But always the physical love between two males must be transcended if real beauty is to be attained. Diotima maintains that a man's life should be spent in contemplation of absolute beauty. Once he has seen that he will not value beauty in terms of gold or rich clothing or of the beauty of boys or young men.[101] The man who sees absolute beauty in its essence pure and unalloyed instead of tainted by human flesh and 'a mass of perishable rubbish', is able to apprehend divine beauty where it exists apart and alone. Such a man will have the privilege of being beloved of God, and becoming immortal if ever a man can be immortal.[102]

Physical love, the female, human childbirth constitute the gross and ugly aspect of life and must be abandoned between male lovers in the attainment of the immortal. It must be noted, however, that when Diotima sets herself the task of enlightening Socrates and leading him to the path of wisdom she makes clear that it is a path which he must follow alone. Diotima merely points the way. She tells Socrates that she will simply tell him of the path and that he must try to follow it.

Diotima, in other words, does not, indeed cannot, lead the way. Her very femaleness, though of a non-sexual kind, debars her from doing so if Plato's notion of eros is to be at all logically consistent. In her female body Diotima necessarily retains her feminine procreative power which is physical in nature. She has a higher degree of perceptiveness than most women and a higher degree, clearly, than some men. She is, however, still biologically a woman, and in the terms in which the ascent to knowledge has been defined, she has not the means of making that ascent. She simply knows of its existence and points the way, indicating that perfect revelation lies at the end of it.

There is no equivalent relationship for women to the love that men have for boys, which would be the first step to philosophy. Love of women for women, like love of men for women, is also an inferior kind of love. This is explained in *The Symposium* by means of the humorous speech of Aristophanes. Aristophanes claims that there were originally three sexes, male, female and hermaphrodite. As a punishment for pride these creatures were cut in two by Zeus and thereafter sought their other half. Those who were halves of hermaphrodites sought women and, Aristophanes maintains, most adulterers come from this class, as do women who are sexually promiscuous.

Those who were halves of a female whole receive scant attention. Aristophanes simply says that Lesbians belong to this category. But those who were halves of a male whole, he says, love men throughout their boyhood and take pleasure in physical contact with them. Such are the best of their generation because they are the most manly.[103] Heterosexual love is debased, lesbian love is dismissed, homosexual eros alone makes the men the best of their generation.

In Aspasia and Diotima Plato has the means of pronouncing on the intellectual potential of women through the mouths of exceptional women. The exceptional woman for Plato is not outstanding simply by virtue of having a greater degree of intellect and ability than most women, but by virtue of her perception of female inferiority and the ultimately masculine nature of true knowledge. Aspasia relegates physical birth to secondary importance to the birth of the community from mother earth. It is the subordination of personal life to the good of the country – a typically masculine value. Diotima has the insight to recognize the all-male character of spiritual love and the subsequent attainment of knowledge. She also has the insight to perceive that attainment of this knowledge is the prerogative of the male. Women may go only so far on the path to knowledge and no further. Diotima herself shrinks from attempting the final stage. For her it is impossible. It is for Socrates to take the last steps alone.

These, then, would be the Guardian women of *The Republic*. By setting aside female sexuality, relinquishing female power and acknowledging the supremacy of masculinity, they would present no threat to the Ideal State.

6 Plato and Feminism

Despite the fairly obvious questions which can be raised concerning the real status of women in the Guardian Class, whether they are genuinely or only superficially equal, and what is Plato's actual perception of their intellectual capacities, his inclusion of women in the Guardian Class has led to much discussion and debate concerning the possibility of a feminist dimension to his political theory.[1] This alleged feminism has rested not only on interpretations of Book V of *The Republic*, but to a certain extent on *The Laws,* where women remain private wives and mothers but are allowed a degree of participation in public life according to ability and once they are beyond childbearing years.[2]

Such interpretations, however, usually overlook the fact that Plato is not at all concerned with the social or political situation of women as such, and he would surely have had to have such considerations in mind in order to conform to any modern definition of feminism. Plato is instead concerned with the welfare of the state as a whole and with methods of attaining political stability within it. Women are considered only in so far as they are a component part of the state whose role, like that of the men, must be clearly defined, and rigidly adhered to thereafter, in the interests of the entire community.

Whatever opportunities Plato provides for the inclusion of women in public life and in the administration of the state, these must be placed in the context of his political theory as a whole. The motivation behind the living and working arrangements of the Guardians does not rest, at the outset, on a notion of the basic inequality of women within society, nor on a consequent belief that something should be done about that inequality.

Plato's theory is not, in fact, based on a belief in individual political rights for either men or women. Indeed, it would be surprising if it were. Plato would have been centuries ahead of his time if he had espoused such notions since in the Athenian society of the fifth century BC the rights accorded to men were not the rights of the individual but the rights of the citizen – an entirely different concept. Not all men were equal as a matter of moral right, and self-fulfilment for the citizen was seen to be through his involvement in the *polis*. It would be strangely inconsistent of Plato to consider extending individual rights to women where they would not have been accorded to some men.

Plato's theory rests on the idea that all social and political arrangements within the state should be for the good of the community. Women are not included in the running of the Ideal State, or of the second-best city which appears in *The Laws*, because Plato believes that it is only morally right that they should have the same opportunities as the men. They are included because he believes that all abilities should be utilized and all members of the community, male or female, should perform their appropriate function within society.

That Plato believes that some women have a certain level of ability cannot be denied, but this is far from believing in the basic tenets of even the broadest definition of feminism.

Plato's belief in the general inferiority of the female, displayed in women's inferiority of soul and lesser capacity to reason, also gives rise to his perception of them as potentially subversive. It makes sense, therefore, for the best of them, those whose abilities can be used, to be integrated into a social situation where they will be subject to the same discipline and control as the men, and their dangerous nature thereby curtailed.

The Ideal State is not founded on a notion of fairness but on a notion of justice. Justice, a moral concept, is fully explained at the beginning of *The Republic* as a prelude to the setting up of the state.

JUSTICE AND EQUALITY IN THE REPUBLIC

The first problem that one encounters in assessing Plato's notion of justice is that the Greek word used in *The Republic* which is generally translated as 'justice' does not, in fact, translate exactly into English. Consequently, justice does not adequately explain what Plato actually means. The Greek word *dikaiosuné* has less a legal and more a moral meaning than the word 'justice' in English. It is the Greek word most generally used for morality.[3]

Dikaiosuné more accurately means 'doing right' and this is a matter of some importance, because what constitutes *dikaiosuné*, 'justice,' or doing right, is the subject of some controversy in the opening passages of *The Republic*. The principal characters themselves cannot agree on a definition, and it is perhaps partly because of this linguistic difficulty that discussions on Plato's supposed feminism have often rested on shaky foundations involving questionable definitions of one kind or another.

For example, Julia Annas argues that it is remarkable, in a work which makes proposals about women as radical as those of *The Republic* and which has so much to say about justice, that inequality of the sexes is not presented as injustice, and that the proposals to treat the sexes equally are not presented as measures which will make the state more just than its rivals.[4]

It is clear from this, however, that Annas is defining justice in a very specific and limited way. She obviously takes justice to mean a notion of fairness, or moral right in terms of the treatment of individuals judged, not on grounds of sex, but simply as human beings. But since Plato would not, and certainly does not, define justice in such a way, his failure to present justice in the state as equality between the sexes is not in the least remarkable. To the contrary, it would have been remarkable if he had made such an assertion.

Definitions of feminism also cause problems. Carol MacMillan, however, argues that the view central to all feminist thinking is that the process of moral argument presupposes the principle that everyone should be treated equally, that they are all rational beings and that there is therefore no moral justification for treating people differently because of their age, sex, intelligence or colour.[5]

Had Plato embraced such a view then both justice and feminism would appear to have been served in the Guardian Class. But Plato's notion of justice does not rest on any such presupposition. What is more, it must not be forgotten that the Guardian Class is one small, elite section of the state. Taken as a whole the state is riddled with inequalities of one kind or another based on age, intelligence and sex. Plato could not, therefore, be called feminist in terms of a definition such as MacMillan's, however general that definition might be.

Plato considers men and women and accords them their position in society, not on the basis of human rights, but in terms of their respective capabilities in performing certain tasks. He does consider what is morally right but he defines what is morally right in terms of the good of the community and not in terms of individuals' rights or interests.

The Republic, a logical construct, poses questions of moral philosophy. It seeks to know what society would be like in ideal and perfect form. It asks what would constitute the best form of government in such a state. That Plato's notion of justice, or 'doing right', in political terms is not a legal but a moral consideration is made clear at the very beginning of the dialogue when Socrates rejects a definition of justice offered by Cephalus, the wealthy old man in whose house the dialogue is set. Cephalus argues that justice is to avoid cheating and lying and to make sure that no debt is left unpaid and no sacrifice to God unmade.[6] It is a definition which is not only legalistic but individualistic. It centres on a notion of honesty in business dealings and on personalized religion, each left to his own conscience and the judgement of God.

Socrates replaces this definition with one of his own which rests not upon the individual's concern for his own well-being during life and after death, but on each performing a special task for which he is fitted. The state, as a consequence, is divided into different classes whose members perform only the tasks for which they are suited. Interference by the classes in each other's jobs and any interchange of jobs between them is forbidden because it would do great harm to the state.

Women find their way into the Guardian Class, not because Plato considers that they should have equal opportunities as human beings, but because he acknowledges that some have the capacities which would be needed by Guardians. In addition to needing such women for the production of superior children Socrates has decreed that justice is served when all potential is fully used in the appropriate position in society. He would be guilty of logical inconsistency were he to exclude women simply on grounds of their sex.

It has already been argued that Plato has other reasons for the inclusion of women among his Guardians. He sees them as less rational and more emotional than men, associated with family life which stands opposed to the public world of politics and which is thereby a threat to the *polis*. The best women who are to be used for breeding purposes are absorbed into a masculine world where they lose their traditional sphere of power and influence and are thereby rendered less dangerous.

But as long as Plato allows these women outlets for their skills, and equality of opportunity with the men, his other motives are not inconsistent with his definition of justice. On the contrary, women's removal from family life serves justice in yet another way. It rids the men of the Guardian Class of distractions which might hinder them from realizing their own full potential.

Plato's notion of justice, then, contains no belief in the fundamental equality of men and women. It rests solely on an equality of capability which, in certain instances, may be similar in the male and the female. This does not mean that Plato sees men and women as being basically the same.

Allen Bloom argues that Plato does not, in fact, believe in the competent woman at all, but fabricates this notion for the purpose of reproducing the Guardian class.[7] Bloom maintains that if the fact that women bear children is to be ignored and does not play a role in their selection as Guardians, if ability is the only criterion, there would be an insufficient number of women in the Guardian Class to reproduce it. It is evident, he says, that women are placed among the Guardians not because they possess the same capacities as men, but precisely because they are different, because they can bear children and men cannot. Maybe, he adds, their souls are the same, but the influence of the body is powerful. The necessity of the body makes justice to souls difficult. Bloom believes, in light of this, that Socrates fabricates a convention about the nature of women in order to legitimate treating women in the same way as men.[8]

But if Bloom is right in this contention it invites the question once again as to why Socrates did not devise some other method of taking care of reproduction which would have excluded women from a role for which they were not fitted. If Plato is effectively lying about his belief in the exceptional woman, he has sabotaged his own ideal state at the outset by placing those who are not fitted to rule in a position where they can. It seems highly unlikely, to say the least, that he would have done so. It would have served no purpose and been potentially damaging. It would, in fact, in terms of his own definition, have failed to attain the Ideal State, and this makes no sense.

Christine Pierce raises the further question as to why Plato should create such a myth about women without telling us that it is a myth as he does in the case of the magnificent myth which explains the distribution of metals in the souls of human beings.[9]

This is a good question. If we are to understand the logic behind the Ideal State, and accept it, we must understand what Plato is about. Why, then, does he not say at some point that women are not really the equals of men but we need them in the Guardian Class for the purpose of reproduction? As with the myth of the metals we can only persuade them to accept the conditions in which they will live if we appear to be giving them some compensations. The real business of ruling will, of course, be in the hands of the men, but the women will not know this. In just the same way that they are told that the choice of mating partners is by lottery (when in fact we know that it is by selection of the rulers), they will be told that the tasks they undertake are essential to the governing of the state.

Such a lie would have the effect of placing the necessary number of good breeders in the Guardian Class. It would also explain to the reader what Plato's real motives were and how exactly the Ideal State would function. But at no point does Plato say, or even hint, that such an arrangement is what he really has in mind.

Bloom is in fact mistaken in his contention that Plato believes, or purports to believe, that the fact that women bear children may be ignored, and plays no part in their selection as Guardians. Insofar as women contribute something to the unborn child Plato admits openly to needing the best women to mate with the best men as often as possible. Women's other talents and abilities will indicate which are the best women who will make the best mothers.

Bloom confuses the role of childbearing in the *The Republic* with that of child*rearing* which is altogether different. Plato does not reject the notion of child*bearing* for his guardian women. It would be impossible to do so while at the same time believing that women affect the character and abilities of the unborn child. But he does reject the notion that childrearing is the specialized task of women simply because they give birth. Children do not have to be brought up by their biological parents. Plato makes clear that the 'bearing and rearing of puppies' does not incapacitate female watchdogs or prevent them carrying out other tasks.[10] So it is with Guardian women. If they are capable of other than domestic tasks, they must not be prevented from performing them. The time-consuming task of rearing the children must consequently be delegated to those of lesser competence in other fields. Guardian women are thereby freed to pursue occupations for which they are qualified.

Bloom's contention that men and women may be the same at the level of their souls but that the necessity of the body makes justice to souls difficult, in fact, turns Plato's notion of body and soul upside down. *The Timaeus* tells us that men and women are different at the level of the soul and that body is a reflection of this difference.[11] In *The Republic*, however, Plato indicates that differences in body and biological function can be overcome to a certain extent. It is the difference of the souls of men and women and the implications this has for their ultimate destiny which cannot be changed or overcome.

Despite their biological difference and the fact that women will usually be physically weaker than men, Plato believes that in certain instances they may be treated the same way with allowances for comparative strength and reproductive function. For example, he stipulates that Guardian women must strip for exercise with the men. They must play their part in war and all other duties of the Guardians. But he adds that since they are the weaker they must be given a lighter share of these duties than the men.[12] With minor adjustments for physical strength the women may do all that the men do to the extent that they are capable.

But the difference of men and women at the level of soul is the difference of the superior from the inferior. Even the best women are inferior to men. While obliging women to contribute their maximum effort, Plato never accords them full equality with men, nor does he suggest that they are the same in all respects. When he allots similar tasks to similar people he makes the point that they must be judged in terms of *kinds* of sameness or difference.[13] He comments that in general the male is better at everything than the female, and excludes cooking and weaving from account on the basis that women are 'thought' to be experts at these and get laughed at if a man does them better.[14] There is at least an implication in this that men could also do those tasks better were they to try.

Justice in *The Republic* does not rest on a notion of equality between the sexes but rather on a notion of the inequality of ability. This applies within the Guardian Class itself and not simply to the differences between the classes. In setting up the Guardian Class in the first place Plato selects his young men and then chooses women to go with them. The male is the yardstick and the position of women is dealt with only after the situation and education of the guardian men has been settled. Plato comments: '. . . maybe it's a good plan to let women come on the stage now, after the men have played their part.'[15] Women are very much in a secondary and supportive position. Only when the duties of the men have been established can the role of women even be discussed.

Even among the Guardians themselves there is division between those who will govern, 'the best of them'[16], and Auxiliaries. And when Plato speaks of the production of children and their removal from their mothers at birth, Socrates tells us that the children of the 'better' Guardians will be taken to a nursery in a separate part of the city while the children of the 'inferior' Guardians, as well as the 'defective' offspring of the others, will be quietly and secretly disposed of.[17]

It is here that the quality of individual souls is of utmost importance. Plato believes that the Ideal State can never come into being until philosophers become kings or kings become philosophers so that political power and philosophy are in the same hands. There are those who are 'naturally' fitted for philosophy and therefore for political leadership. The rest should follow their lead, but are not to involve themselves in philosophy.[18]

The philosophical nature is one in which there is passion for every kind of wisdom. The philosopher is possessed of knowledge, not mere opinion; physical pleasures will pass him by, and his mind will have a grace and sense of proportion which will naturally and easily lead it to see the Form of each reality.[19]

According to Socrates the philosophic nature, properly taught, will develop every excellence. So the philosophic soul is the soul which contains most of the notion of Form, which is transcendent and which perceives the absolute. It is the masculine soul, the superior sort, which falls in earthly existence into the body of a male. The inferior sort which have seen less of the celestial vision, the less philosophical or non-philosophical souls, are those which end up in the body of a woman. According to this, philosophy and political leadership naturally fall to men. For Plato, women and philosophy are contradictory terms.

Those critics who argue that this cannot be the case as Plato says explicitly that some of the rulers will be women overlook one small but important qualification. For while Socrates certainly does say, 'all that I have said about men applies equally to women',[20] he also adds, if they have 'the requisite natural capacities'.[21] But the requisite natural capacities spring from the philosophical soul, a soul which no woman possesses.

This, once again, is a matter of logical consistency. Justice in the Ideal State requires that all those capable of any task be allowed to perform it. Having included women in the Guardian Class on the basis that childbearing does not in itself affect women's abilities in other directions, Plato has placed them among the elite group from which Rulers must be chosen. Logically, if women had the necessary capacity for philosophy and political leadership, they would have to be allowed to exercise those in the interests of the community. It would constitute injustice, according to Plato's own definition, not to allow them to do so. But in practice this will not occur because the nature of women, even the best women, springs from a soul which is characteristically inferior to that of men. If women cannot be philosophers they cannot be rulers. Justice in the state requires that masculinity rules because masculinity constitutes the superior form of humanity. When Socrates says that women will rule 'if' they are able to do so he feels secure in the knowledge that they are not.

FEMINISM AND THE REPUBLIC

But to suggest that Plato had any notion of feminism in his political theory is, in any case, rather in the nature of an anachronistic argument. It has already been pointed out that definitions of feminism rest on notions which did not appear in political thought until centuries after Plato, and it would have been unlikely for Plato to have considered ideas which centred on the individual and individual rights. The good of the community being the focus of Plato's attention, women, like men, are considered only in so far as they contribute to that end.

Nevertheless, there are those who attempt to read into Plato's practical arrangements for women an implication that he was making such arrangements with some idea of equal opportunities for women in mind. The most positive statement of this kind in recent years was made by Gregory Vlastos who, addressing the question 'Was Plato a Feminist?' in a lengthy and detailed article, concluded that Plato's affirmation of feminism within the Guardian class of the *Republic* is the strongest ever made by anyone in the classical period.[22]

Vlastos proceeds to defend this position by analyzing the situation of the Guardian women in terms of the rights of persons. Acknowledging that Plato's 'feminism' is a controversial subject, he argues that clarity of definition is essential. In order to define feminism he cites a proposed Amendment to the United States Constitution in the early 1980s. This Amendment states that equality of rights under the law shall not be denied or abridged by the U.S. or by any state on account of sex. Vlastos adapts this so that it will cover, he maintains, all personal rights that may be claimed for women – not just the legal ones envisaged by the Amendment but social, economic and moral rights as well. His final definition is: 'Equality in the rights of persons shall not be denied or abridged on account of sex.'

Plato, says Vlastos, will qualify as a feminist if his ideas, sentiments and proposals for social policy are in line with this definition. On this basis he maintains that while the position of the majority
of free women in the ideal state, composing its industrial and agri-
cultural class, is unambiguously anti-feminist, and the position of
the free women in the *Laws* is a hybrid, feminist in some respects
and anti-feminist in others, the position of women within the Guardian Class in unambiguously feminist.

There are two major flaws in this argument. First of all, and by
virtue of Vlastos' own qualification, the argument is only valid if
we adopt the definition of feminism which has been offered. But
why should we – especially when Plato himself would not have done?
It is clear that no such notion is involved in his theory.

Secondly, if one does accept a definition which involves a notion
of equal rights for men and women, Plato could surely only be
feminist or not. There is no intermediate position. According to
Vlastos' reading Plato is feminist, anti-feminist and a mixture of
the two all at the same time. This is impossible if he is to be logically consistent.

Vlastos' acknowledgement that Plato's position regarding women
alters from dialogue to dialogue, or from situation to situation within
one dialogue, is evidence enough that it is not based on a notion
of female rights. If Plato had been thinking in such terms he would
surely have had to arrive at some consistent, philosophically coherent position on the subject.

Vlastos is among those critics who are guilty of adopting an anachronistic argument. He takes a 20th century notion of feminism
and superimposes it on Athenian society in the fifth century BC.
But this will not do, for there is no reason whatever to suggest
that Plato regarded women as an oppressed group within society
and sought to remedy this.

Vlastos goes on to justify his argument by listing in detail the
'rights' which were accorded to the Athenian male in Plato's day
but which were denied to the female. These, he says, would not be
denied to women within the Guardian Class. But he considers such
rights from the point of view of the women concerned and the
effect that such innovations would have on their lives. This was not
a consideration for Plato. He considered women, like men, in terms
of the contribution they could make and not in terms of any so-
called 'rights' they might receive.

As an example of equal rights Vlastos cites education and argues that the schools, gymnasia and palaestrae in Plato's day were a male monopoly. In *The Republic* access would be the same for women Guardians down to the last detail – exercising naked with the men. The reason for this, he maintains, is that the Greeks thought total nudity in athletics a salient feature of their Hellenic culture. To deny it to females, therefore, would be discriminatory.

But the point of similar education for males and females in the Guardian Class is that they must be trained from the earliest age to fulfill their potential and become good Guardians. What is essential training for men is essential training for women where they are to do the same job. Physical education for women is not, therefore, instituted so that the Guardian Class shall be seen to be non-discriminatory on grounds of sex. It is a purely functional arrangement.

Discrimination operates within the Ideal State not on the basis of sex but of ability. Children who do not show early potential, male and female alike, are demoted out of the Guardian Class to fill their appropriate role elsewhere in society. Children of the third class who show potential may be promoted to Guardian status. Plato accepts that while women are in general inferior to men, certain women have abilities which extend beyond the limits of their role in family life. They must be allowed to use those abilities and they must, therefore, undergo any necessary training to enable them to do so whatever that role involves. He makes clear that the Guardians require the best education of the body as well as of the mind. No-one is to laugh at women exercising nude because they do it for 'excellent reasons' and they will be clothed in their own excellence.[23]

When considering women and the right to vocational opportunity Vlastos points out that no gainful employment was open to all women in Athens, except prostitution. Working class women had certain options. They were employable, for example, as midwives, wet-nurses or vegetable sellers. In *The Republic* careers for highest talent are open to women as well as men. Both sexes qualify on equal terms for admission to Guardianship and thereby to all other progressions contained within that job – including the military and the political.

But once again, to imply from this that Plato is a feminist is to suggest that he makes such provisions out of a sense of fairness to talented women who have hitherto not had the benefit of such opportunity. This fails to take account of the element of compulsion which operates in the Ideal State. Able women are not allowed to enter the same professions as men as a matter of moral right, they are obliged to do so as a matter of civic duty.

The Philosopher King has the right to command everyone in the city and everyone must fulfil their prescribed role. This applies to those of the highest as well as the lowest rank. In just the same way that children may be promoted or demoted to any position in society which befits their capabilities, so also the Guardians when they have attained the true vision of reality and have ascended from the dark cave of ignorance and into the sunlight of truth are compelled to return to the cave which constitutes society, despite their desire for a life of philosophy. To the objection that this condemns the intellectual to a poorer life Plato replies that the object of the legislation is not the special welfare of any particular class in society, but society as a whole, and persuasion or compulsion may be used to unite the citizens and make them share the benefits which each, individually, can confer on the community.[24]

Sentiment and personal preference do not belong in the Guardian class. It is the same for women as for men and for philosophers. There is less of an option and more of an obligation in their inclusion in the same occupations as men. Whether talented women would choose to stay in the home is not a consideration. Such a choice does not exist. Women do not have a right to choose to be traditional wives and mothers any more than they have a right to vocational opportunity. They are to obey the command of the Philosopher King.

Vlastos also sees feminist thinking in that certain rights which he feels men have enjoyed previously are taken from them in the Guardian Class, thereby once again making men and women the same. The examples he cites here are the ownership of property and the right to sexual choice. Women, he says, have previously not been allowed to own or dispose of property. Within the Guardian Class property ownership will be denied to both sexes, and public support will be equally assured to both.

In the matter of sexual choice, he points out, women in Athens had little choice about who or when they would marry. Heterosexual intercourse outside marriage was strictly forbidden and there were severe penalties for infringement of the law. Constraints of this sort did not apply to men.

However, in the Guardian Class the interdict on sexual intercourse outside the eugenic unions is the same for men and women while they are of childbearing years. After that sexual liberty is the same for both. He concludes that the double standard of sexual morality is wiped out.

But in both cases that Vlastos has cited, property ownership and sexual behaviour, Plato's reasoning has nothing to do with equality. It has to do with what he perceives to be justice. Property ownership is not denied to both male and female because Plato thinks it is an injustice that the female has previously been excluded from property ownership, but because private ownership of any kind, including that involved within the family in terms of wives and children, is the cause of quarrels and legal disputes.

This happens when members of a society no longer agree on the use of the words 'mine' and 'not mine', and Plato concludes that the best ordered state is one in which as many people as possible use these words in the same sense of the same things.[25] It is to facilitate this end that everything must be held in common by the Guardians, including wives and children. The lack of private ownership in the Guardian Class will, thereby, see an end to litigation.

Unanimity is the greatest good a society can enjoy, and Plato maintains that as a result of the laws concerning property and family the Guardians will live in complete peace with each other. If they do not quarrel amongst themselves there will be no danger of rebellion or faction in the rest of the community.[26] It is the stability of the state which is served by the property laws.

On the question of sexual conduct, Plato's primary concern, having done away with the family, is to find a means of reproducing the best children to repopulate the elite class. The introduction of mating festivals means that women will exchange a sexual relationship with one man and a personal relationship with their own children for occasional partners chosen for them by the rulers and the possibility of different partners at different festivals.

But while it is true to say that this means the male Guardians' sexual conduct is regulated in a way that has not hitherto been the case, Plato nevertheless makes provision for the best of them to sleep more frequently with women as a reward for distinguished service in war and other activities. Sexual reward takes its place among 'other honours' that young men may win.[27]

While Plato indicates that this is actually a pretext to ensure that the best Guardians mate most often with each other, the 'reward', as it is to be deemed, is explicitly for the men. Sexual intercourse remains a duty for the women. There is nowhere any suggestion that women should be allowed to sleep more frequently with the men as a reward for distinguished service, though in a state where both men and women perform the same tasks, including military ones, the opportunity to distinguish themselves would exist for women as well as for men. Plato does not appear to consider this possibility. Sexually, women in the Guardian Class remain in a subordinate situation to men, part of their function the sexual gratification of the male, and part the production of the best children. There is no question here of a double standard having been eliminated. It simply exists in accordance with a different set of rules from those traditionally imposed by the institution of marriage.

Sexual liberty beyond childbearing years is for those Guardians who have not become Philosophers. Those who have will necessarily have risen beyond the need for physical gratification. Those who have not, may mate as they please because this no longer has any relevance to the state. It cannot undermine it by the production of inferior children. Women, who do not have philosophical souls and who are always associated with the flesh can, when their reproductive life is over, provide an outlet for the continuing sexual needs of inferior Guardians, an outlet that cannot be satisfied in any other way since Plato stipulates that homosexual intercourse will be against the law. Older men, he makes clear, may only express as much affection for boys as would a father for his son. Young men, still potentially capable of the ascent to philosophy, must not be corrupted.[28]

Women's sexuality is, in fact, largely irrelevant and completely ignored within the Guardian Class. Only their reproductive capacity is important to the state and this is curtailed and confined within rules which define legitimacy in terms of sacred mating festivals instead of marriage vows. Whether women wish to extend their sexuality to a multiplicity of partners or to give up their children at birth is not a consideration. Only the welfare of the state is important.

Plato does not consider the lives of women as women but only as another factor which must be taken into account when devising the best social and political system which will create stability and order in the city. He is not concerned with the rights of persons or with equality between the sexes. He is concerned with justice, and he has defined justice in a very clear and specific way.

THE RELATIONSHIP BETWEEN *THE REPUBLIC* AND *THE LAWS*

In *The Laws* families are not abolished and women remain private wives and mothers to their own children. This is one of the main distinctions affecting the lives of women between this dialogue and *The Republic*. But while the family is the foundation of the state, women are not confined to their domestic role. At certain times of their lives they may undertake administrative tasks. They are also included in military training, and girls receive the same education as the boys.

In the light of this Trevor Saunders points out that the apparent difference between *The Republic* and *The Laws* in terms of the development of Plato's political theory has prompted the comment that as Plato grew older his optimism turned to pessimism, his idealism to realism. Saunders rightly rejects this view on the basis that it confuses the attainable with the unattainable.[29]

The whole point about the political arrangements in *The Republic* is that they constitute the arrangements which would be necessary to attain the *ideal* state. Nowhere is there the suggestion that Plato thinks that such arrangements, however desirable or morally sound, are a practical possibility. It is *The Laws* which presents a view of a *real* republic in its best form, and Plato's view of women's appropriate situation appears, at first sight, to have undergone a considerable change. They are no longer to be released from domestic tasks and the strictures of childbearing so that they might concentrate all their efforts on suitable careers for which an early education, equal to that of men, might qualify them. They are, to a certain extent, to fulfil a dual function, performing their traditional duties within the family and contributing outside it to a limited extent where possible. Family life, however, has undergone a significant change in *The Laws*.

Marriage and 'related topics' are the subject of wide-ranging legislation. Everything from choice of partners, (for example, a headstrong person should marry a quiet one in the interests of harmony and balance), to correct procreation and the registration of births and deaths is considered a suitable subject for the rule of law. And Plato makes one very important, over-riding stipulation: 'We should seek to contract the alliance that will benefit the state, not the one that we personally find most alluring.'[30]

As in *The Republic* the good of the state takes precedence over personal life and marriage must be contracted in accordance with this principle. The family is clearly not to centre on the good of its members in the traditional way, but to make its contribution as a component part of the city in whose life everyone is involved. Family in *The Laws* is to function much in the same way as the Guardian Class does in *The Republic*.

Even the law concerning dowries is designed to minimize individual family concerns. Plato tells us that if the poor have to marry, or give away in marriage, on limited resources this will not affect their prospects of a long life because public provision will ensure that no-one in the state is to go without the necessities of life.[31]

In terms of this reconstructed image of family life, then, women will have some outlets for other than domestic talents. However, to suggest that this contains elements of feminism, though in less than ideal form, or to argue as Vlastos does that this arrangement is a hybrid, feminist in some respects and anti-feminist in others, is to presuppose once again that Plato embraces some notion of fair treatment of women as a matter of correcting a social injustice. This is no more Plato's intention in *The Laws* than it is in *The Republic*.

In *The Laws* he emphasizes that education is to be compulsory for one and all. But this is because children belong to the state first and to their parents second. He stresses that this applies to girls as well as boys, and goes on to say that they must be trained in precisely the same way without any reservations about horse-riding or athletics being suitable for males but not females.[32] But while Plato speaks of women being placed in this way in a position of 'equality' with the men, he also makes his motivation for this step quite clear. His reasons parallel those of *The Republic* in terms of utilizing all the state's best potential. It is for the good of the community and not for the purpose of elevating the status of the female that Plato believes in equal education. Almost every state, he tells us, develops only half its potential, whereas with the same cost and effort it could double its achievement. He considers this a 'staggering blunder' for a legislator to make.[33] He points out that under the Spartan system girls are trained in athletics but do not have any military service. This means, he says, that in an emergency which led to a battle for the state and for the lives of their children they would be unable to take up shield and spear to defend their native land. It is his conclusion that the legislator must not stick at half measures of this sort and allow women to 'wallow in expensive luxury'. This gives the state only half the loaf of prosperity instead of the whole of it.[34]

At no point does Plato suggest that female potential is exactly the same as men's or that they are equal in all respects and that, therefore, to educate them equally will make the state more just. Defence of the city and the use of all talent are Plato's motives throughout.

Susan Moller Okin argues that neither equality nor liberty nor justice in the sense of fairness were values for Plato. The three values on which his ideal and second-best cities were based were harmony, efficiency and moral goodness.[35]

Moral goodness, of course, in Plato's terms *is* the good of the state and female potential, like male potential, is used to that end. In the light of this Okin questions what the actual position of women in *The Laws* will be. The fact that they are still to be private wives, she points out, curtails their participation in public life in more ways than one.

As regards military training Okin points out that for all Plato's assertion about the necessity of training women in defence of the state, they are in fact allowed, not compelled, to train up to the age of twenty, and then excluded from military service until they are past childbearing. They are exempted again at fifty. Since men were to have no other sexual outlets than their wives, and since contraception was not in an advanced state, this could mean an expectation of only five years of military service from adult women.[36]

Okin argues further that since women in *The Laws* are once more private wives, unable to control their pregnancies which would be controlled for them in *The Republic*, this would further curtail their participation in public life. She concludes that despite Plato's professed intention to emancipate women and make use of their talents, his reintroduction of the family has the direct effect of putting women firmly back into their traditional place.[37]

But Plato, in fact, neither says nor infers that he wishes to 'emancipate' women. He simply points to the value to the state of using all potential, including female potential. And while Okin is right to argue that women are still largely in their traditional role, their participation in political life to any degree at all places the female role, and consequently the role of women in family life, in a different perspective.

The inclusion of women in public life serves other purposes than those served by simply utilizing all available talent. The situation of women in *The Laws* is once again similar to that in *The Republic* in that it educates women to think and behave like men and accept masculine principles and a masculine view of the world.

Plato's view of female nature in its natural and uneducated form is given clear expression at other points in the dialogue. For example, when speaking of the Persian Monarchy under Cyrus, Plato comments that Cyrus was a good commander but never considered the problem of education or the running of a household. As a result he handed over the children to the women to bring up. The women of the royal harem, left alone without men, consequently gave the children a 'womanish' education, one characterized by pampering and indulgence. The outcome of this was that when Cyrus' children came to their inheritence, they were living in 'a riot of unrestrained debauchery', driven by intolerance and lack of self-control.[38] A womanish education, then, unrestrained by the hand of the male, is not simply inadequate, it is disastrous. Cyrus' children end up dead or deposed.[39]

Likewise, when Plato discusses music as artistic representation he points out that it requires careful handling, and a man who goes wrong on the subject suffers a good deal of harm and is attracted to evil dispositions. The reason for this is that the authors of such music have not the same degree of creative ability as the actual muses. The muses, he says, would never make the ghastly mistake of composing the speech of men to a musical idiom suitable for women. Neither would they fit rhythms appropriate to the portrayal of slaves to the tune and bodily movements of free men.[40]

Women are categorized here with those of humble and inferior status, just as they are in *The Republic* when Plato points out that the greatest variety of desires and pleasures and pains, those things which must be overcome by the Guardians, are to be found in children, women and slaves and in the less respectable majority of so-called free men.[41]

That female nature must be subject to control is made clear when Plato discusses the setting up of communal meals for men and women. Citing once again the laws of Sparta, he points out that the Spartans had a system of communal meals for men but did not include women. This was entirely wrong, he says, because it left half the human race to its own devices. That half was the female sex, that which was inclined to be secretive and crafty because of its weakness.[42]

The state, thereby, lost control of a great many things which ought to have been regulated by law. Leaving women to their own devices was not just to lose half the battle:

a woman's natural potential for virtue is inferior to a man's, so she's proportionately a greater danger, perhaps even twice as great.[43]

Women, then, are a potential danger to the state because the state's virtue may be compromised by those with an inferior capacity for that particular excellence. The happiness of the state will be better served, Plato concludes, if all arrangements apply to men and women alike.[44] He clearly believes that whatever capacity women do have for virtue will be developed through the contact they will have with the superior sex. Left to their own devices, the inferior side of their threatening nature will prevail.

Equal treatment, once again, does not signify equality of the sexes. Equality, like virtue, has a special meaning for Plato. In just the same way that he refers to 'kinds' of sameness and difference in *The Republic*, so also equality has to be judged in terms of 'kinds' of equality.

Plato explains that even if you proclaim that a master and his slave shall have equal status, friendship between them is inherently impossible. The same thing applies to the relations between an honest man and a scoundrel. Indiscriminate equality for all amounts to inequality, and both fill a state with quarrels between its citizens.[45]

While Plato does not explicitly mention equality between the sexes, his reference to the inferior virtue of women, and his occasional references to them in the same category as slaves, indicates that his argument may reasonably be taken to extend to any notion of equality between men and women. It is fundamentally not possible.

Plato goes on to argue that there are two concepts of equality and that they are virtual opposites. The first is the kind which applies to weights, measures and numbers. Determining this is within the competence of any state or legislator. The second, the 'most genuine' and best kind of equality is not so easily arrived at. It takes the wisdom and judgement of Zeus.

The general method of attaining this kind of equality, Plato explains, is to grant much to the great and less to the less great, adjusting what is given to take account of the real nature of each. More specifically, one should confer high recognition on great virtue, but as to the poorly educated in this respect, one should treat them as they deserve.[46]

According to this argument women, whom Plato has already relegated to the status of the less virtuous, will receive as much equality as they deserve. It is, in fact, a similar equality to that which they will receive in the Ideal State, though Plato is more obscure about his intentions in *The Republic* than he is in *The Laws*. Women are granted equality according to their abilities but the highest status of Philosopher King is for the men who have philosophical souls. Women receive only as much equality as they deserve in accordance with the amount of virtue they possess.

This is spelled out more clearly in *The Laws*. Women are given their appropriate role in society, one which uses as much of their potential as possible while at the same time keeping them in subordination to the male and to ideals of masculinity.

Statesmanship, Plato maintains, consists essentially in strict justice. The Legislator must always make this his aim ' . . . and this is precisely as we've described it: it consists of granting the 'equality' that unequals deserve to get.'[47]

Plato's view of women in *The Laws* is not inconsistent with that of *The Republic*, and neither is feminist. While in the Ideal State Plato would rupture all ties with family life for his Guardians, his purpose in doing so is the good of the state, served by making those of highest talent fulfil their appropriate role. That some talented women may show Guardian potential and must cease to be private wives and mothers does not alter the fact that it is men, not women, whom Plato releases from the stricture of family since it is men, not women, who have the highest capacity for virtue and who will become Philosopher Kings. They must consequently be placed in an environment which is protected from the worst aspects of family and female nature, so that their full potential may be realized.

In *The Laws* Plato acknowledges that such arrangements are not a practical possibility and consequently allows women as much public life as is consistent with their simultaneously retaining their roles as wives and mothers in an adapted form of family. But in both cases the equality granted to women is the degree of equality which is consistent with what Plato perceives to be the inherent inequalities in human beings and the inherent differences between men and women.

Conclusion: A Return to the Gender Debate

I have argued throughout that Plato's philosophy is a gendered philosophy, that its very basis – a belief in absolutes, Forms which constitute every excellence – is masculine in nature. What is more, Plato's idea of masculinity contains within it a corresponding notion of femininity, the male and female deriving their identity from a relationship to one another. The relationship is one of opposition, it is that of the superior male to the inferior female.

For Plato, it is the male which is associated with the Forms, with rational thought and with order and restraint. It is the female which is associated with Prime Matter, with the physical, the emotional and with disruption and chaos. Consequently, it is the superior male which must dominate the threatening female.

I have argued also that such fundamental aspects of Plato's philosophy are relevant to his political theory. For while Plato appears to allow women an equality of opportunity and participation in political life in his Ideal State, and allows them a degree of political participation in the second-best city, his motivation rests on masculine ideals, and not on a belief in the essential equality of men and women. A notion of the supremacy of the universal over the particular, the public over the private, and the good of the community rather than the individual, governs the political arrangements of both ideal and second-best cities, and in accordance with such principles women have public status to the extent that they are capable of emulating masculinity, subduing femininity and thereby negating the threat which the female, in her traditional role, presents to the masculine world of politics.

The significance of such conclusions, however, is not restricted to an understanding of Plato, nor do I believe that his attitudes concerning male and female nature belong strictly within the confines of his abstract Ideal State, frozen in time and with no relevance to the modern day.

True, Plato's theory is set in Athens in the fifth century BC. This seems very far removed from the modern western world and there might well exist the temptation to discount the possibility of its having any contemporary relevance. I believe, on the contrary, that views such as those expressed by Plato, however long ago they were first articulated, are still crucial to modern feminist debate. For the questions Plato asks concerning women and politics, women and rational thought, women and reproduction, remain controversial. They are at the heart of any philosophical enquiry into sexual identity and consequently they are at the centre of the many practical problems which women continue to encounter in their daily lives, in both public and private spheres.

Women are still seriously under-represented, not only in active politics, but in practically every profession, most particularly in senior positions. And arguments to the effect that fewer women than men are to be found at the top level in political or business careers because they simply do not seek office, and that this reflects a 'natural' disinclination, women continuing to put family first, will no longer do. Enough research has been done in recent years concerning women in all areas of public life to show that if fewer seek a high profile, or at least fail to attain it, it is usually because of the obstacles they must overcome and the choices and sacrifices they are called upon to make. It is not because of their belief in their innate inferiority, nor is it a lack of ambition which causes the shortfall.

And the obstacles which exist, alongside prescriptions concerning women's appropriate role in society, though they may be superficially of a practical or conventional nature, can actually be seen to be grounded in fundamental notions of gender, of what is considered to be the 'natural' role for the male and the female. Ingrained prejudices contained within such perceptions of gender roles are not easily removed.

It is twenty years since Jean Baker Miller argued that the question was still asked of women: 'How do you propose to answer the need for child care?' This, she argued, was an obvious attempt to structure conflict in old terms. The question, she suggested, should be: 'If we as a human community want children, how does the total society propose to provide for them?'[1] Two decades later and the question is still seldom posed in this way; far less is it satisfactorily answered.

Yet it is a vital question. The greater provision of childcare facilities, maternity benefits, and the greater involvement of men in the matter of childrearing, continue to be problematic regardless of the concept of the 'new age man', depicted 'holding the baby', involving himself more in the family than have previous genera-

tions. The reality is that women are still generally seen as responsible for family matters, though more men may help out more than
they used to. 'Househusbands' and 'role reversal' situations are still
more novel than commonplace.

Feminists, of course, have argued for years that the care and
welfare of children is not, and should not be, the responsibility of
the biological mother alone, but the concern of the community,
and that it is not the case that one sex, albeit the sex that physically gives birth, is naturally suited to the task of upbringing. Much
has been said of the unfairness of a social system which has been
based on biological function and which discriminates in all sorts of
ways against one gender.

But the problems surrounding sexual identity and social equality
remain largely unresolved and all avenues of research seem to return to the original starting point – the question of what is and is
not 'natural' in the male and female. If there are differences in the
nature of men and women, what exactly are they? Are they, indeed, related to their biological function, or can this be totally ignored in evaluating the reasoning capacities or the talents or
capabilities of men and women?

The solution to this dilemma, and the development of feminist
perspectives in philosophy and political theory, does then require
more than simply identifying misogyny or unfair treatment of women
in past philosophies, important as this might be. It requires an evaluation of the very definition of femininity within those philosophies
and an assessment of how those definitions might be challenged.

Plato's inclusion of women in the Guardian Class and the terms
upon which he includes them – the abolition of marriage and family, the sacrifice of their own children – invites precisely this challenge. Those terms indicate that Plato's definition of femininity did
not embrace the able woman at all.

Only those who are perceived to be unfeminine women, whose
childbearing capacity does not interfere too much with their rational thinking, are included in his political theory. Had Plato had a
different view of femininity, one which valued female attributes and
associated feminine perspectives with intellectual ability, one can
only conjecture what the role of women in his Ideal State would
have been. It would certainly have had to be different, and Plato's
political theory would have been a very different theory.

In this connection Prudence Allen's theoretical framework,
incorporating sex unity, sex polarity and sex complementarity,

is particularly relevant as two of these positions are consistent with the political arrangements of the Ideal State. Only one is problematic.

Allen has argued that Plato is a sex unity theorist, that he believes in the fundamental sameness, and therefore equality, of men and women at the level of their souls. According to this belief men and women may be treated in the same way.

I have argued, rather, that it is a unity of masculinity and not sex neutrality which prevails in the Ideal State. Men and women are treated in the same way in that women are treated like men, which is possible only when they have stepped outside their childbearing role. This role is minimized and they are placed in a similar situation to men so that they may absorb the standards of masculinity. Nevertheless, the political arrangements of the Ideal State still make perfect sense in terms of sex unity theory.

They are, however, equally coherent in terms of sex polarity, which position, I believe, more accurately reflects Plato's true belief about the nature of men and women. For Plato, men and women are essentially different at the level of their souls. However, in certain instances they may be treated in the same way so that the adverse effects of femininity, and the dangers which are caused by the ways in which men and women are different, may be eliminated from the elite Guardian class. This also makes perfect sense. So two very different views of women might lead to a similar political system.

But in neither case has the problem of sexual identity been resolved. In both cases the supremacy of masculinity remains, and what is characteristically feminine is that which must be jettisoned in the attainment of knowledge.

This cannot, and does not, apply where sex complementarity is concerned. If Plato had embraced a notion such as this, had he believed that not only were men and women fundamentally different, but that they were also genuinely equal, then the political arrangements of the Ideal State could not have been as they were. Plato could not have eliminated femininity from his Guardian class while at the same time defining it in terms of having an equal contribution to make to society. In accordance with Plato's own definition of justice, which involves everyone making their maximum contribution to the state in the role for which they are best fitted, different arrangements would have had to be made for women if women had a peculiarly female contribution to make. Equality for women would have had to be equality of another kind than effectively turning them into surrogate men.

This, of course, raises the question as to what sort of political arrangements would create real equality in terms of sex complementarity theory. It is all very well to criticize theorists, including some feminist theorists, for failing to take account of women's special difference, particular attributes, essential nature, without attempting to define exactly what these are, and without explaining their special relevance. Allen herself makes the point that no attempt has as yet been made to do this in such a way as would give complementarity theory a firm philosophical foundation.

It is certainly the case that some feminist theorists have avoided the issue by putting forward arguments for what appears to be a sex neutral, non-gendered, form of humanity. But, on closer inspection, this has often seemed to defeat the whole point of 'feminism'. If one flattens out all characteristics seen to be peculiarly feminine and, for example, removes women from the exclusively female function of childbearing, with all its attendant psychological and emotional experience, it might well be argued that the battle to find a space for women as women in an equal, rather than a male-dominated world, has been lost at the outset.

It is interesting that Firestone's revolutionary plea for childbirth to be taken over by technology appears to have fallen on deaf ears. In more than two decades since this was written there has been no noticeable clamour from women begging to have the physical experience of birth removed from their lives. To the contrary, the more sophisticated technology involving reproduction becomes, the more it appears to be sought by women hitherto unable to have their own children, wishing to give birth naturally. Where there has been controversy it has usually surrounded cases such as those where women far beyond normal childbearing years, some of them over sixty years of age, have been given medical assistance to produce their own children.

Most recently, much publicity has been given to the case of the young widow fighting a court battle to be allowed access to her late husband's sperm in order to give birth to his child, having been denied this on the legal technicality that he did not give written consent before he died.

The evidence would appear to suggest, in other words, that women, regardless of any other aspirations or ambitions they may have, still seek to fulfil their maternal role. And while it may be argued that this desire is, in itself, socially constructed, there is no real evidence for saying that even if this were largely true it constitutes the whole story.

It has always seemed to me that to pursue arguments which either neglected to take account of women's vital human experience, or attempted to deny this altogether, might place women in the dangerous position of fighting their way out of the woods only to find themselves marching towards a cliff.

But the problem is how this experience is to be conceptualized and formulated into some valid philosophical position. Lloyd, acknowledging this problem, points out that women cannot be easily accommodated in a cultural ideal which has defined itself in opposition to the feminine.[2] A further problem, she adds, is that philosophers in western tradition have been predominantly male, and the female philosophers there have been have been philosophers in spite of, rather than because of, their femaleness. Consequently, there has been no input of femaleness into the formulation of ideals of Reason.[3]

Women, clearly, have come a long way since the Athens of Plato's day, though not as far or as fast as many of us would have wished. The story so far has been challenging and fascinating but frustrating too. Like any good thriller it has pointed to a variety of solutions, and then tantalized us by revealing some of them to be red herrings, Plato's inclusion of women in the Guardian Class possibly being the most famous and influential red herring of them all.

But where do we go from here? If we pursue a general theory of humanity which applies to both men and women, excluding any consideration of gender, we confront at once the obvious problems of essentialism.

Carol Gould has argued very persuasively that to cite gender as an 'accidental' difference between human beings – and therefore not one relevant to philosophical debate – is in any case an impossible position to sustain. Essentialists, she says, cannot distinguish between 'essential' and 'accidental' properties. To do this they would have to be able to recognize what was the same in all human cases, what was different in all human cases and what was different between human and non-human cases. Her point is that if the essentialist cannot claim to distinguish in every case between what is essential and what is accidental, one could not know that being human is, in itself, essential and that being differentiated by sex is accidental.[4]

The question, of course, is not so much whether it is possible, or whether it is necessary, to take as one's starting point the essential non-gendered human being, in analysing men and women in the world, but rather whether it is at all relevant.

Thinkers throughout a history of political thought who have wished to consider 'natural man', logically abstracted from society, acknowledged that the state of nature might never have existed historically, and if it had we could not know about it. An obvious point of criticism, therefore, is the one which questions the relevance of such a state of nature for men who are, in fact, living in society.

Much the same argument might be offered in the case of gender. Since human beings are differentiated in this way and since we do not exist in a vacuum but in relationship to other human beings, male and female alike, it is only in this context that the significance of gender to rational thinking can be analysed. And it is surely possible to do this without lapsing into some crude 'biology is destiny' type of argument.

De Beauvoir's argument for androgyny may have been flawed, but her contention that women will always have a different relationship to their bodies, to men and to children, than men have to their bodies, to women and to children, is on a much surer footing. It acknowledges the role of direct human experience in shaping the way we think, and in this context a woman's way of looking at the world may be as relevant as that of a man, though entirely different. Or, in the interests of equality, and to avoid using the male once again as the yardstick by which rational thinking is measured, a man's way of looking at the world may be as relevant as a woman's – though very different. For the problem is not a matter of finding a way to obliterate differences but of understanding and possibly even appreciating them – and this is a two-way street. Masculinity and femininity will always stand in relation to one another. It is the nature of the relationship which needs to be explored more fully. A complementarity theory would wish to change the perception of the relationship from one of opposition to one of mutual support, and this is possibly the most positive way forward. Allen herself sees it as the only really fruitful line of enquiry left.

One is tempted to give the last word on the matter back to the ancient Greeks. In *The Symposium* Aristophanes' comic portrayal of human beings, punished by the gods for some offence, split in two halves and eternally seeking their other half, is as poignant as it is funny. Love seeks fulfilment, it seeks completeness. One half, of course, by definition, is always equal to the other.

References

CHAPTER 1   THE GENDER DEBATE

1. Considerable work has been done over the past two decades on the subject of gender in philosophy and feminist critique of philosophical tradition. For example: Carole Gould, *The Woman Question: Philosophy of Liberation and the Liberation of Philosophy* (Philosophical Forum, Vol. 5, 1973–74); C. Gould and M. Wartofsky (eds), *Women and Philosophy: Towards a Theory of Liberation* (Pedigree Books, New York, 1976); L Clark and L Lange (eds), *The Sexism of Social and Political Theory: Women and Reproduction from Plato to Nietzsche* (University of Toronto Press, Toronto, 1979); Janet Radcliffe Richards, *The Sceptical Feminist: A Philosophical Inquiry* (Routledge & Kegan Paul, Boston, 1980); Hester Eisenstein, *Contemporary Feminist Thought* (George Allen & Unwin, 1984); Marilyn Pearsall (ed.), *Women and Values* (Wadsworth Publishing, California, 1986); Morwenna Griffiths and Margaret Whitford (eds), *Feminist Perspectives in Philosophy* (Macmillan Press, Hampshire, 1988); Karen Green, *The Woman of Reason* (Polity Press, Cambridge, 1995); Julie K. Ward (ed), *Feminism and Ancient Philosophy* (Routledge, London, 1996); Evelyn Fox Keller and Helen E. Longino, *Feminism and Science* (Oxford University Press, Oxford, 1996).
2. Elizabeth V. Spelman, *Woman as Body: Ancient and Contemporary Views* (Feminist Studies 8, no. 1, Spring 1982), p. 109.
3. See, for example, *The Republic* 605d, where Socrates expresses the view that men should bear grief in silence, and while they may be carried away by their feelings while watching dramatic poetry on stage, in private lives such behaviour is 'womanish'. Likewise *The Phaedo* 115d–17a where Socrates shames his young companions for their tears on the basis that this is why he had the women removed from his death cell.
4. See Lefkowitz and Fant, *Women's Life in Greece and Rome* (Duckworth, London, 1982), pp. 82–4.
5. Machiavelli, *The Prince* (Penguin Classics, Middlesex, 1961), p. 133.
6. Jean-Jacques Rousseau, *The Social Contract & Discourses*, (J.M. Dent & Sons Ltd, London, 1973).
7. Jean-Jacques Rousseau, *Emile* (J.M. Dent & Sons Ltd, Cambridge, 1966).
8. Mary Wollstonecraft, *Vindication of the Rights of Woman* (Penguin Classics, Middlesex, 1975).
9. Jean Grimshaw, *Feminist Philosophers: Women's Perspectives on Philosophical Traditions* (Wheatsheaf Books, Hertfordshire 1986), p. 3.
10. Spelman, p. 109.
11. Grimshaw, p. 3.

12. Genevieve Lloyd, *The Man of Reason* (Methuen & Co, London 1984), p. ix.
13. Ibid., p. ix.
14. Ibid., p. ix.
15. Aeschylus' *Eumenides* begins with a chorus of 'Furies' or 'Erinyes' called upon by Clytemnestra to pursue her son Orestes who has been responsible for her death. In his introduction to the *Eumenides* Herbert Weir Smith describes them as 'a band of fearsome creatures who wish to avenge all who shed kindred blood.' See Aeschylus, *Eumenides*, Loeb Classical Library, 1926).

Cults associated with fertility and earth goddesses, and the significance of these in Greek literature, are discussed by Jane Ellen Harrison in *Themis: A Study of the social origins of Greek Religion* (Cambridge University Press, Cambridge, 1912). Harrison argues that the chorus of Furies in the *Eumenides* represents more than a prologue. It sets forth the notion of conflict between the old social order of the *daimones* of the Earth – represented by matriarchy or a matrilinear system – and the *theoi* of Olympus, Apollo and his father Zeus who represent patriarchy. Harrison traces a sequence of cults which existed at Delphi and argues that they represented a transition from Gaia, or Earth, to Apollo. This transition, she claims, was seen as a fight between Earth and Sun, between Darkness and Light, between 'the dream oracle and the truth of heaven.' See *Themis* pp. 385–93.
16. Lloyd (1984), p. 2.
17. Carol MacMillan, *Women, Reason & Nature* (Basil Blackwell, Oxford, 1982), pp. 55–6.
18. Ibid., p. 52.
19. Ibid., pp. 55–6.
20. Diana Coole, *Women in Western Political Theory: From Ancient Misogyny to Contemporary Feminism* (Wheatsheaf, Sussex, 1988), p. 1.
21. Lloyd (1984), p. 3.
22. Coole (1982), p. 1.
23. Ibid., p. 2.
24. Ibid., p. 2.
25. Ibid., p. 3. Coole acknowledges here that in regard to those whom she terms more radical thinkers, it would be 'churlish' to deny that feminism has made some gains. She cites Socrates, Plato, Augustine, Wollstonecraft, Marx and Engels among those thinkers who have adopted a 'prima facie' radical position. She maintains, however, that their demands for sexual equality have, on closer inspection, been seen to involve the rejection of all things feminine.
26. Ibid., p. 3.
27. Ibid., p. 4.
28. Simone de Beauvoir, *The Second Sex* (Penguin Books, Middlessex, 1949), p. 13.
29. Grimshaw (1985), p. 16. In a critique of de Beauvoir, Carol Ascher makes a similar point. She comments: '. . . in reading *The Second Sex*, one is often left with the unhappy question: why can't a woman be

more like a man?' See Ascher, *Simone de Beauvoir: A Life of Freedom* (Harvester Press, Brighton, 1981), p. 150.
30. Prudence Allen, *The Concept of Woman: The Aristotelian Revolution, 750 BC – AD 1250* (Eden Press, Quebec, 1985), p. 3.
31. Ibid., p. 5.
Allen cites Hildegard of Bingen (1098–1179), author of the earliest known morality play, *Ordo Virtutum*, as the foundress of sex-complementarity. She argues that while a notion of sex complementarity had been expanding through a number of monasteries within the Benedictine tradition from the ninth to the twelfth centuries, Hildegard was the first philosopher to articulate a complete theory of sex complementarity. Allen maintains that this theory is not completely consistent but that it covers all four categories of the concept of women in relation to the concept of man – opposition, generation, wisdom and virtue. For a full discussion of Hildegard's theory see Allen pp. 292–315.
32. Ibid., p. 4.
33. De Beauvoir (1949), p. 14.
34. Ibid., p. 15.
35. Ibid., p. 16.
36. Ibid., p. 737.
37. Ibid., p. 735.
38. Grimshaw (1985), p. 46.
39. De Beauvoir (1949), p. 740.
40. Ibid., p. 740.
41. Ibid., p. 740.
42. Shulamith Firestone, *The Dialectic of Sex: The Case for Feminist Revolution* (Women's Press, London, 1979), p. 192.
43. Ibid., p. 224.
44. Ibid., p. 215.
45. Ibid., pp. 188–90.
46. Jeffner Allen, *Motherhood: The Annihilation of Women*, in *Women and Values*, Marilyn Pearsall (ed.), (1986), p. 91.
47. Ibid., pp. 91–2.
48. Ibid., p. 92.
49. Firestone (1979), pp. 189–90.
50. Adrienne Rich, *Of Woman Born* (Virago, London, 1977), p. 13.
51. Ibid., pp. 39–40.
52. Coole (1988), p. 240.
53. Prudence Allen (1985), pp. 292–315.
54. Spelman (1982), pp. 110–11.
55. Ibid., p. 110.
56. See, for example, Susan Moller Okin, *Women in Western Political Thought* (Virago, London, 1980). Okin acknowledges that in Plato's youthful environment there was a trace of radical thought about women overlying a strong tradition of misogyny. She adds, however, that the prevailing depiction of women in the Platonic dialogues is extremely deprecating and indicates the author's belief in the innate inferiority of the female. Plato, she says, shared his fellow Athenians' contempt for the women of his day.

See also Sarah Pomeroy, *Goddesses, Whores, Wives and Slaves* (Schocken Books, New York, 1975), pp. 117–118. Referring to misogyny in classical literature, and the limited lives of Athenian women, Pomeroy comments that Plato's provision for female Guardians in his proposed ideal state is remarkable. But she adds that it cannot be regarded as undiluted feminism. She argues that Plato did not believe that women in general were the equals of men, and points out that he repeatedly classified women with children. This, she says, may have been because wives were often only fourteen years old. Among those critics who maintain that Plato was a feminist are Richard Crossman and Gregory Vlastos. In *Plato Today* (Unwin Books, London, 1937) Crossman argues that Plato is a feminist because he wanted to free women from the bondage of marriage and from the ambitions which that bondage imposed upon them. However, he also acknowledges that part of Plato's reason for doing so was that the women of the ruling class had to be worthy partners for the men. See Crossman pp. 122–23. Vlastos claims that in terms of equal rights Plato's affirmation of feminism within the Guardian Class is the strongest ever made by anyone in the classical period. See *Was Plato Feminist?* Times Literary Supplement (March 17–23, 1989).

57. Ellen Kennedy and Susan Mendus (eds), *Women in Western Political Philosophy* (Wheatsheaf Books, Sussex, 1987), p. 21.

58. See Wendy Brown, 'Supposing Truth were a Woman' (*Political Theory,* Vol. 16, No. 4, November 1988).

See also Arlene Saxonhouse, *Women in the History of Political Thought* (Praeger Publishers, New York, 1985) Chapter 3.

59. I.M. Crombie, *An Examination of Plato's Doctrines* (Routledge & Kegan Paul, London, 1962), pp. 9–11.

60. See *Symposium* (Penguin Classics, Middlesex, 1951) 208c–209e and 212c.

61. Crombie (1962), p. 11.

CHAPTER 2   THE MASCULINE SOUL

1. Plato, *The Republic* (Penguin Classics, Middlesex, 1955) 514b–16c.

2. Plato, *Phaedrus* (Penguin Classics, Middlesex, 1973) 247.

3. Ibid., 247–49.

4. Crombie (1962), p. 293.

5. G.M.A. Grube, *Plato's Thought* (Athlone Press, London, 1980), p. 120.

6. Ibid., p. 121.

7. Ibid., p. 122.

8. Plato, *Timaeus* (Penguin Classics, Middlesex, 1965), p. 30.

9. Plato, *Phaedrus*, 245.

10. Ibid., 246.

11. Plato, *Laws* (Penguin Classics, Middlesex, 1970) 892.

12. Ibid., 892.

13. Plato, *Laws*, 895.

14. Plato, *Republic*, 442b.

15. See Allen, *The Concept of Woman* (1985), p. 80.

16. Plato, *Republic*, 454d.
17. Ibid., 455e.
18. Ibid., 455d.
19. Ibid., 455d.
20. Ibid., 442b.
21. Ibid., 444b.
22. Ibid., 395e.
23. Ibid., 605e.
24. Plato, *Phaedrus*, 246.
25. Ibid., 247.
26. Ibid., 250.
27. Ibid., 248–49.
28. Plato, *Republic*, 617e.
29. Ibid., 618b.
30. Ibid., 415b–15d.
31. Plato, *Timaeus*, 35.
32. Ibid., 35.
33. Ibid., 41.
34. Ibid., 42.
35. Ibid., 42.
36. Ibid., 91.
37. Ibid., 42.
38. Ibid., 42.
39. Allen (1985), pp. 58–60.
40. Ibid., pp. 58–60.
41. Ibid., p. 81.
42. Plato, *Timaeus*, 42.
43. Allen (1985), pp. 60–1.
44. Ibid., p. 59.
45. Ibid., p. 59 & *Timaeus*, 51b.
46. Ibid., p. 59 & *Timaeus*, 50c.
47. Ibid., p. 60.
48. Ibid., p. 60.
49. Plato, *Republic*, 454e.
50. Allen (1985), p. 61.
51. Ibid., p. 61.
52. Plato, *Timaeus*, 42.
53. Plato, *Republic*, 454e.
54. Ibid., 454d.
55. Ibid., 395e.
56. Plato, *Phaedrus*, 248.
57. Ibid., 251–52.
58. Ibid., 246.
59. Ibid., 246.
60. Ibid., 251.
61. Ibid., 250.
62. Ibid., 246.
63. Ibid., 247.
64. Ibid., 246.

65. Ibid., 249.
66. Ibid., 251.
67. Ibid., 251.
68. Ibid., 251.
69. Ibid., 254.
70. Plato, *Timaeus*, 48.
71. Ibid., 69.
72. Ibid., 69.
73. Ibid., 90.

CHAPTER 3   THE TRANSCENDENT MALE

1. Michel Foucault, *The History of Sexuality* (Penguin Books, London, 1976), p. 61.
2. Evelyn Fox Keller, *Reflections on Gender and Science* (Yale University Press, New Haven, 1985), p. 19.
3. Plato, *Phaedrus*, 251.
4. Plato, *Symposium*, 207b.
5. Ibid., 208c.
6. Plato, *Timaeus*, 48.
7. Saxonhouse (1985), p. 50.
8. Ibid., p. 50.
9. Plato, *Republic*, 455c.
10. Plato, *Menexenus* (Loeb Classical Library, 1930), 237d/e.
11. Keller (1985), p. 24.
12. Hans Kelson, *Platonic Love* (in *American Imago*, Vol. 3, 1942), p. 28.
13. Ibid., p. 29.
14. Plato, *Lysis*, 204c.
15. Plato, *Phaedrus*, 240.
16. W.H.D. Rouse, *Great Dialogues of Plato* (Plume, London, 1970), p. x.
17. K.J. Dover, *Greek Homosexuality* (Duckworth, London, 1978), p. 23. Dover points out that the law cited in the case of Timarchus referred specifically to the 'sale' and not the 'gift' of one's body. The case did not say anything about 'unnatural practices' or 'gross indecency'. Thus, he concludes it appeared not to impose penalties on those who submitted to homosexual acts for love or for fun.
18. Aeschines, *The Speeches of Aeschines* (trans. C.D. Adams, Loeb Classical Library, 1919), 11–15.
19. Dover (1978), p. 103.
20. Plato, *Lysis*, 206a.
21. Plato, *Symposium*, 218d.
22. Ibid., 218d.
23. Ibid., 219e.
24. Dover (1978), p. 90.
25. Ibid., p. 67.
26. John J. Winkler, *The Constraints of Desire* (Routledge, London, 1990), p. 45.
27. Ibid., p. 46.

28. Ibid., p. 46.
29. Plato, *Symposium*, 217b.
30. David Halperin, *One Hundred Years of Homosexuality* (Routledge, London, 1990), p. 97.
31. Plato, *Republic*, 403c.
32. Ibid., 442.
33. Ibid., 461b/c.
34. Plato, *Laws*, 839.
35. Ibid., 839.
36. Winkler (1990), p. 18.
37. Ibid., p. 18.
38. Keller (1985), p. 2.
39. Plato, *Republic*, 458d.
40. Ibid., 460b.
41. Ibid., 540b.
42. G. Lowes Dickinson, *Plato and His Dialogues* (Pelican Books, Middlesex, 1947), p. 136.
43. Plato, *Phaedrus*, 237.
44. Ibid., 238.
45. Ibid., 238.
46. Ibid., 241.
47. Ibid., 241.
48. Ibid., 244.
49. Ibid., 246.
50. Ibid., 247.
51. Ibid., 247.
52. Ibid., 249.
53. Ibid., 249.
54. Ibid., 249.
55. Ibid., 251.
56. Ibid., 250–51.
57. Ibid., 251.
58. Keller (1985), p. 24.
59. Plato, *Phaedrus*, 251.
60. Ibid., 251.
61. Ibid., 254.
62. Ibid., 254.
63. Ibid., 254.
64. Ibid., 255.
65. Ibid., 256.
66. Ibid., 256.
67. Ibid., 256.
68. Ibid., 256.
69. Plato, *Symposium*, 191c.
70. Kelson (1942), p. 21.

CHAPTER 4   THE IMMANENT FEMALE

1. Plato, *Timaeus*, 46.
2. Lloyd (1984), p. 5.
3. Okin (1980), p. 15.
4. Spelman (1982), p. 113.
5. Ibid., p. 113.
6. Coole (1988), pp. 1–2.
7. Ibid., p. 3.
8. Ibid., p. 3.
9. Plato, *Republic*, 458c.
10. Ibid., 459a–60c.
11. Coole (1988), p. 41.
12. Plato, *Republic*, 401c.
13. Ibid., 464a.
14. De Beauvoir (1949), p. 44.
15. Lefkowitch and Fant, *Women's Life in Ancient Greece and Rome* (Duckworth, London, 1982), p. 85.
16. Ibid., p. 41.
17. Ibid., p. 95 (from Hippocrates *On Virgins*).
18. Ibid., p. 96 (from Hippocrates, *Nature of Women*, 8.3).
19. Ibid., p. 96. Hippocrates, *Aphorisms*, also comments on the significance of blood to women's physical and mental state: 'If a woman vomits blood, this ceases with the onset of menstruation', and: 'It is a sign of madness when blood congeals about a woman's nipples.' (See *Aphorisms*, 32 and 40, in *Hippocratic Writings*, Lloyd (1950).
20. Lefkowitch, *Heroines and Hysterics* (Duckworth, 1981), p. 13.
21. Sarah B. Pomeroy, *Goddesses, Whores, Wives and Slaves* (Schocken Books, New York, 1975), p. 118. *In Sexual Life in Ancient Greece* (1935), Hans Licht quotes Euripides as saying that it was 'highly wrong' to join together two young people of the same age because the strength of the man lasts far longer than the beauty of a female which passes away more quickly (Licht, p. 40).
22. Xenophon, *Oeconomicus*, VII.10.
23. Helen King, *Bound to Bleed* (in *Images of Women in Antiquity*, Cameron and Kuhrt (eds), Croom Helm, Kent, 1984), p. 111.
24. Xenophon, *Oeconomicus*, IX.19.
25. Lefkowitch (1981), p. 15.
26. Lefkowitch & Fant (1982), pp. 94–5.
27. Ibid., pp. 94–5.
28. Lefkowitch (1981), pp. 16–17.
29. Plato, *Timaeus*, 91.
30. Ibid., 91.
31. Coole (1988), p. 19.
32. Ibid., p. 17. The *Oresteia* is a trilogy which tells the story of the murder of Agamemnon by his wife, Clytemnestra. Their son, Orestes, slays his mother to avenge his father but is in turn pursued by the female Erinyes from the Underworld who punish murders of kin. The god Apollo purifies Orestes on the basis that the crime is a justifiable one,

and conflict erupts between Apollo and the Erinyes. Coole argues that the heart of the conflict is the question as to whether matricide or homicide is the greater crime and therefore whether blood-bond or bed-bond, kinship or legal relations, mother-right or father-right takes precedence. (Coole, p. 18).

33. Ibid., p. 19.
34. Plato, *Symposium*, 208c.
35. Page duBois, *Sowing the Body* (University of Chicago Press, Chicago/London, 1988), pp. 169–83.
36. Ibid., p. 173.
37. Ibid., p. 173.
38. Plato, *Phaedrus*, 251.
39. Ibid., 254–56.
40. Plato, *Symposium*, 208c.
41. Ibid., 208c.
42. Spelman (1982), p. 119.
43. Plato, *Republic*, 455c/d, *Meno*, 73.
44. Spelman (1982), p. 115.
45. Plato, *Laws*, 944e.
46. Ibid., 945.
47. Spelman (1982), p. 117
48. Plato, *Laws*, 917.
49. Ibid., 781.
50. Spelman (1982), p. 117.
51. Ibid., p. 118.
52. Plato, *Phaedrus*, 251.
53. Spelman (1982), p. 119.
54. Plato, *Timaeus*, 42.
55. Plato, *Phaedo*, 57c–9e.
56. Ibid., 57c–9e.
57. Ibid., 62e–4a.
58. Ibid., 64b–5c.
59. Ibid., 65c–6e.
60. Ibid., 65c–6e.
61. Ibid., 67a–8b.
62. Ibid., 67a–8b.
63. Ibid., 115d–17a.
64. Ibid., 114a–15d.
65. Ibid., 117a–18.
66. Plato, *Last Days of Socrates* (Penguin Classics, 1954), p. 199.
67. Plato, *Phaedo*, 81d–3a.

CHAPTER 5   THE NATURE OF WOMEN AND THE WORLD OF POLITICS

1. In speaking of 'Athenian wives' I am aware that I am restricting the discussion to certain women of a particular social standing. Not all women in classical Athens were respectable matrons. There were also

slaves, flute girls, prostitutes and hetairai. Sarah Pomeroy's history of women in antiquity, *Goddesses, Whores, Wives and Slaves*, covers all categories and indicates how wide-ranging an inquiry into the lives of women in general requires to be. The purpose here, however, is to investigate the role of women in Plato's political thought and consequently I have concentrated on the category of women from which Plato's exceptional women would most likely be drawn. In terms of education and opportunity women of Guardian potential would most often be found among the wives and mothers or potential wives and mothers of Plato's own class.

2. Hans Licht, *Sexual Life in Ancient Greece* (George Routledge & Sons, London, 1935), p. 28.
3. T.B.L. Webster, *Life in Classical Athens* (B.T. Batsford, London, 1969), p. 34.
4. H.D.F. Kitto, *The Greeks* (Pelican Books, Middlesex, 1951), p. 223.
5. Ibid., pp. 223–6.
6. Licht (1935), p. 28.
7. Kitto (1951), p. 230.
8. Ibid., p. 226.
9. Ibid., p. 233.
10. A.W. Gomme, *Essays in Greek History and Literature* (Basil Blackwell, London, 1937), p. 101.
11. Aristophanes, *Lysistrata, Acharnians, Clouds* (Penguin Classics, Middlesex, 1979); *Lysistrata*, 1141.
12. Ibid., 528.
13. Dover (1978), p. 11.
14. Aristophanes, *Lysistrata*, 489.
15. Xenophon, *Oeconomicus* (Loeb Classical Library edition, trans. E.C. Marchant and O.J. Todd, 1923), p. 135.
16. Ibid., pp. 425–9.
17. Ibid., 429.
18. Kitto (1951), p. 221.
19. Ibid., p. 221.
20. A.E. Taylor, *Plato: The Man and His Work* (Methuen, London, 1978), p. 2.
21. David Schaps, *Economic Rights of Women in Ancient Greece* (Edinburgh University Press, Edinburgh, 1979), pp. 4–7.
22. Ibid., pp. 4–7.
23. Ibid., p. 14.
24. Ibid., p. 57.
25. Philip Slater, *The Glory of Hera* (Beacon Press, Boston, 1971), p. 8.
26. Ibid., p. 8.
27. Ibid., pp. 28–9.
28. Webster (1969), pp. 46–7.
29. Grube (1980), pp. 87–8.
30. Pomeroy (1975), p. 93.
31. Ibid., p. 93.
32. Ibid., p. 93.
33. Ibid., p. 94.

34. Ibid., p. 97.
35. Homer, *The Odyssey* (trans. Walter Shewring, Oxford University Press, Oxford, 1980), p. 137.
36. Saxonhouse (1985), p. 28.
37. Euripides, *Medea and Other Plays* (Penguin Classics, Middlesex, 1963); *Electra*, 1009–42.
38. Saxonhouse (1985), p. 29.
39. Lefkowitch, in *Images of Women in Antiquity* (Cameron and Kuhrt, eds, 1984), p. 50.
40. Ibid., pp. 50–1.
41. Aristophanes, *Lysistrata*, 95.
42. Ibid., 209.
43. Ibid., 1–45.
44. Ibid., 528.
45. Aristophanes, The *Assemblywomen* (Penguin Classics, 1978), 968–1117.
46. Saxonhouse (1985), p. 36.
47. Jean Bethke Elstain, *Public Man, Private Woman* (Martin Robertson & Co, Oxford, 1981), p. 11.
48. Ibid., p. 12.
49. Ibid., p. 16.
50. Ibid., p. 16.
51. Grimshaw (1986), pp. 17–18.
52. Plato, *Republic*, 401c/d.
53. Ibid., 465d/e.
54. Lefkowitch and Fant (1982), pp. 82–4.
55. Plato, *Timaeus*, 91; *Republic*, 414b–15c.
56. Plato, *Republic*, 415c.
57. Ibid., 459e.
58. Ibid., 460d.
59. Homer, *Odyssey* (trans. Shewring, 1980), 197–278.
60. Mary O'Brien, *The Politics of Reproduction* (Routledge & Kegan Paul, London, 1981), p. 37.
61. Ibid., 123.
62. Plato, *Republic*, 462c.
63. Ibid., 464a.
64. Ibid., 464a.
65. Ibid., 461b.
66. Ibid., 461.
67. O'Brien (1981), p. 124.
68. Plato, *Symposium*, 202a. Socrates tells us here that what he says of love was taught to him by Diotima, a woman of Mantinea.
69. Eva Canterella, *Pandora's Daughters* (John Hopkins University Press, London, 1981, English trans. 1987), p. 55.
70. Plato, *Symposium*, 202a.
71. Dover (1968), p. 161.
72. Ibid., p. 161.
73. Halperin (1990), pp. 129–130.
74. Ibid., p. 130.
75. Dover (1978), p. 67.

76. Winkler (1990), pp. 48–50.
77. Plato, *Symposium*, 217b.
78. Ibid., 218d.
79. Ibid., 218d.
80. Ibid., 218d.
81. Plato, *Phaedrus*, 255.
82. Plato, *Menexenus*, 236c.
83. Plato, *Symposium*, 205e.
84. H.D. Rankin, *Plato and the Individual* (Methuen, London, 1964), p. 96.
85. Plato, *Symposium*, 208c.
86. Plato, *Menexenus*, 237c.
87. Ibid., 237c.
88. Plato, *Republic*, 414e.
89. Plato, *Menexenus*, 237d/e.
90. Ibid., 237d/e.
91. Ibid., 237d/e.
92. Saxonhouse (1985), p. 56.
93. Ibid., p. 56.
94. Ibid., p. 55.
95. Plato, *Symposium*, 203b.
96. Plato, *Symposium*, 208c.
97. Ibid., 209e.
98. Ibid., 209e.
99. Ibid., 211a.
100. Plato, *Phaedrus*, 249.
101. Plato, *Symposium*, 211a–12c.
102. Ibid., 212c.
103. Ibid., 191c.

CHAPTER 6   PLATO AND FEMINISM

1. The question of Plato's feminism has stimulated a number of articles. These include: Christine Garside Allen, *Plato on Women* (Feminist Studies Vol. II, 1975) and *Can a Woman be Good in the Same Way as a Man?* (Dialogue, Vol. 10, 1971); Julia Annas, *'Plato's Republic and Feminism'* (*Philosophy*, Vol. 51, 1976); Anne Dickason, *Anatomy and Destiny: The Role of Biology in Plato's View of Women* (Philosophical Forum, Vol. 5, 1–2, 1973–74); Christine Pierce, *Equality: Republic V* (The Monist, Vol. 57, 1973); Arlene Saxonhouse, *The Philosopher and the Female in the Political Thought of Plato* (Political Theory, Vol. 4, 1976).

   Most feminist theorists dispute the contention that Plato is feminist though some argue that a notion of femininity is to be found in his philosophy. Arlene Saxonhouse, for example, argues that Plato introduced a notion of politics which centred on maternity rather than paternity. (Saxonhouse, *Women in a History of Political Thought*, p. 56.) Likewise, Wendy Brown in *Supposing Truth were a Woman* (Political Theory, Vol. 16, no. 4, Nov. 1988), comments that the 'sexing' of an important strain of Plato's epistemology does not mean he is a feminist but she adds that he nevertheless engages in a critique of male modes of thinking, speaking and acting. (p. 594).

I have concentrated in this chapter on the arguments of Gregory Vlastos in *Was Plato Feminist?* (Times Literary Supplement, March 17–23, 1989) as Vlastos is the most recent scholar to make the positive assertion that Plato is a feminist, at least in terms of the proposals for the Guardian Class of the *Republic*.

2. See Plato, *Laws* Book Six, 780–85.
3. See Plato, *Republic* (Penguin Classics, trans. Desmond Lee, p. 65).
4. Julia Annas, *Plato's Republic and Feminism* (1976), p. 314.
5. MacMillan, *Women, Reason and Nature* (1982), p. ix.
6. Plato, *Republic*, 331b.
7. Allen Bloom, *The Republic of Plato: An Interpretative Essay* (New York Basic Books, New York, 1968), p. 383.
8. Ibid., p. 383.
9. Pierce, *Equality: Republic V* (1973), p. 10.
10. Plato, *Republic*, 451d/e.
11. Plato, *Timaeus*, 91.
12. Plato, *Republic*, 457b.
13. Plato, *Republic*, 454b.
14. Ibid., 455c/d.
15. Ibid., 451c.
16. Ibid., 412c.
17. Ibid., 460c.
18. Ibid., 473d.
19. Ibid., 485–87.
20. Ibid., 540c.
21. Ibid., 540c.
22. Vlastos, *Was Plato Feminist?* (TLS 1989), p. 276.
23. Plato, *Republic*, 457a/b.
24. Ibid., 519e/520.
25. Ibid., 462c.
26. Ibid., 465b.
27. Ibid., 460b.
28. Ibid., 403c.
29. Plato, *Laws* (Penguin Classics, trans. Trevor Saunders), p. 27.
30. Ibid., 773.
31. Ibid., 774.
32. Ibid., 804.
33. Ibid., 805.
34. Ibid., 806.
35. Okin (1980), p. 28.
36. Ibid., p. 49.
37. Ibid., p. 50.
38. Plato, *Laws*, 694–5.
39. Ibid., 695.
40. Ibid., 669.
41. Plato, *Republic*, 431c.

42. Plato, *Laws*, 781.
43. Ibid., 781.
44. Ibid., 781.
45. Ibid., 757.
46. Ibid., 757.
47. Ibid., 757.

CONCLUSION

1. Jean Baker Miller, *Towards a News Psychology of Women* (Pelican, Middlesex, 1976), p. 134.
2. Lloyd (1984), p. 104.
3. Ibid., p. 105.
4. Gould (1973), p. 6.

Bibliography

Aeschines	*The Speeches of Aeschines* trans. C.D. Adams Loeb Classical Library, 1919
Aeschylus	*Eumenides, Agamemnon, Libation Bearers, Fragments* trans. Herbert Weir Smith Loeb Classical Library, 1926
Allen, C. Garside	*Can a Woman be Good in the Same Way as a Man?* Dialogue, Vol. 10, 1971
Allen, Prudence	*The Concept of Woman: The Aristotelian Revolution* Eden Press, Quebec, 1985
Annas, Julia	*Plato's Republic & Feminism* Philosophy, 51, 1976
Arendt, Hannah	*The Human Condition* Chicago University Press, Chicago, 1958
Aristophanes	*The Knights, Peace, The Birds, The Assemblywomen, Wealth* trans. Alan H. Sommerstein, Penguin Classics, Middlesex, 1978
	Lysistrata, Acharnians, Clouds trans. Alan H. Sommerstein, Penguin Classics, Middlesex, 1979
	The Wasps trans. Douglass Parker, Mentor Books, New York, 1962
Aristotle	*The Generation of Animals* trans. A.L. Peck Loeb Classical Library, 1943
	Nicomachean Ethics trans. H. Rackham Loeb Classical Library, 1935
Ascher, Carole	*Simone de Beauvoir: A Life of Freedom* Harvester Press, Brighton, 1981
Barker, Ernest	*Political Thought of Plato & Aristotle* Russell & Russell, New York, 1959
Blok, Josine & Peter Mason	*Sexual Asymmetry* J.C. Gieben, Amsterdam, 1987

Bloom, Allen	*The Republic of Plato: An Interpretative Essay* New York Basic Books, New York, 1968
Bluestone, N.H.	*Women and the Ideal Society* Berg Publishers, Oxford, 1987
Brown, Wendy	*Supposing Truth were a Woman* Political Theory, Vol. 16, No. 4, November, 1988
Cameron, Averil & Amelie Kuhrt (eds)	*Images of Women in Antiquity* Croom Helm, Kent, 1984
Canterella, Eva	*Pandora's Daughters* John Hopkins University Press, London, 1981 (English trans. 1987)
Chadwick J. & M. Mann	*Medical Works of Hippocrates* Basil Blackwell, Oxford, 1950
Chetwynd, Jane & Oonagh Hartnett	*The Sex Role System* Routledge & Kegan Paul, London, 1978
Chodrow, Nancy	*The Reproduction of Mothering* University of California Press, London, 1978
Clark, L. & L. Lange	*The Sexism of Social and Political Theory: Women and Reproduction from Plato to Nietzsche* University of Toronto Press, Toronto, 1979
Coole, Diana	*Re-reading Political Theory from a Woman's Perspective* Political Studies, Vol. 34, No. 1, March, 1986
	Women in Political Theory Wheatsheaf, Brighton, 1988
Cooper, David	*The Death of the Family* Penguin Books, Middlesex, 1971
Cornford, Francis M.	*The Republic of Plato* Oxford University Press, 1977
Crombie, I.M.	*An Examination of Plato's Doctrines* Routledge & Kegan Paul, London, 1962
Crossman, R.H.S.	*Plato Today* Unwin Books, London, 1937
de Beauvoir, Simone	*The Second Sex* Penguin Books, Middlesex, 1949
Dickason, Anne	*Anatomy and Destiny: The Role of Biology in Plato's View of Women* Philosophical Forum, Vol. 5, Nos 1–2, autumn/winter, 1973–74
Dickinson, G. Lowes	*Plato and His Dialogues* Pelican Books, Middlesex, 1947

Dinnersterin, Dorothy *The Mermaid and the Minotaur*
Harper Colophon, New York, 1976

*The Rocking of the Cradle and the
Ruling of the World*
Souvenir Press, London, 1978
Diogenes Laertius *Lives of Eminent Philosophers*
trans. R.D. Hicks. Loeb Classical
Library, 1925
Dover, K.J. *Greek Homosexuality*
Duckworth, London, 1978

*Greek Popular Morality in the
Time of Plato & Aristotle*
Basil Blackwell, Oxford, 1974
duBois, Page *Sowing the Body*
University of Chicago Press,
Chicago/London, 1988
Ehrenberg, Victor *The People of Aristophanes*
Basil Blackwell, Oxford, 1943
Eisenstein, Hester *Contemporary Feminist Thought*
George Allen & Unwin, London, 1984
Elshtain, Jean Bethke *Against Androgyny*
Telos, 47, Spring, 1981

Moral Woman and Immoral Man
Politics and Society 4, summer, 1975

Public Man, Private Woman
Martin Robertson & Co, Oxford, 1981

*The Feminist Movement & the Question
of Equality*
Polity 7, summer 1975
Euripides *Iphigenia in Taurica*
trans. Arthur S. Way, Loeb Classical
Library, 1916

Medea and Other Plays
Penguin Classics, Middlesex, 1963
Evans J. (ed.) *Feminism and Political Theory*
Sage, London, 1986
Finley, M.I. *Democracy Ancient and Modern*
Chatto & Windus, London, 1973

Politics in the Ancient World
Cambridge Univerisity Press, Cambridge, 1983

The Ancient Greeks
Chatto & Windus, London, 1963
Firestone, Shulamith *The Dialectic of Sex*
Women's Press, London, 1979

Foley, Helen P.	*Reflections of Women in Antiquity* Gordon & Breach, London 1981
Foucault, Michel,	*The History of Sexuality* Penguin Books, Middlesex, 1979
Friedan, Betty	*The Feminine Mystique* W.W. Norton, New York, 1963
Friedlander, Paul	*Plato: An Introduction* Routledge & Kegan Paul, London, 1958
	Plato: The Dialogues, Second and Third Period Routledge & Kegan Paul, London, 1969
Friedrich, Paul	*The Meaning of Aphrodite* University of Chicago Press, London, 1978
Gilligan, Carol	*In a Different Voice* Harvard University Press, Cambridge, Mass., 1982
Gilman, Charlotte Perkins	*The Man-Made World* Source Books Press, New York, 1970 (reprint of 1911 edition)
Gomme, A.W.	*Essays in Greek History & Literature* Basil Blackwell, London, 1937
Gould, Carole	*The Woman Question: Philosophy of Liberation and the Liberation of Philosophy* Philosophical Forum, Vol. 5, no. 1–2, autumn/winter, 1973–4
Gould, C. & M. Wartofsky	*Women and Philosophy: Towards a Theory of Liberation* Pedigree Books, New York, 1976
Gould, Thomas	*Platonic Love* Routledge & Kegan Paul, London, 1963
Green, Karen	*The Woman of Reason* Polity Press, Cambridge, 1995
Griffiths, Morwenna & Margaret Whitford	*Feminist Perspectives in Philosophy* MacMillan Press, Hampshire, 1988
Grimshaw, Jean	*Feminist Philosophers: Women's Perspectives on Philosophical Traditions* Wheatsheaf Books, Sussex, 1986
	Review of *Women, Reason & Nature* (by Carol MacMillan), Radical Philosophy, no. 34, London, 1983
Grube, G.M.A.	*Plato's Thought* Athlone Press, London, 1980
Gunnell, John G.	*Political Theory: Tradition & Interpretation* Winthrop Publishers, Cambridge, Mass., 1979

Guthrie, W.K.C.	*The Greeks & Their Gods* Methuen, London, 1950
Hall, Dale	*The Republic and the Limits of* *Politics* Political Theory, Vol. 5, No, 3, August, 1977
Halperin, David	*One Hundred Years of Homosexuality* Routledge, London, 1990
Hardie, Amy	*Review of Women, Reason & Nature* (by Carol MacMillan) Radical Philosophy, No. 34, London, 1983
Harrison, Jane E.	*Themis: A Study of the Social Origins* *of Greek Religion* Cambridge University Press, London, 1912
Holmans, Hilary	*The Sexual Politics of Reproduction* Gower Publishing, Aldershot, 1985
Homer	*The Iliad* trans. Lord Derby J.M. Dent, London, 1948
	The Iliad: A New Prose Translation trans. Martin Hammond, Penguin Classics, Middlesex, 1987
	The Odyssey trans. Walter Shewring, Oxford University Press, Oxford, 1980
Irigaray, Luce	*Speculum of the Other Woman* trans. Gillian C. Gill, Cornell University Press, New York, 1985
Keat, Russell	*Masculinity in Philosophy* Radical Philosophy, Vol. 34, London, 1983
Keller, Evelyn Fox	*Reflections on Gender and Science* Yale University Press, New Haven, 1985
Keller, Evelyn Fox & Helen E. Longino	*Feminism & Science* Oxford University Press, Oxford, New York, 1996
Kelson, Hans	*Platonic Love* In American Imago, Vol. 3, 1942
Kennedy, Ellen & Susan Mendus (eds)	*Women in Western Political Philosophy* Wheatsheaf Books, Sussex, 1987
Kerenyi, C.	*The Gods of the Greeks* Thames & Hudson, London, 1951
Kitto, H.D.F.	*The Greeks* Pelican Books, Middlesex, 1977
Kuhn, Annette & Marie Wolpe	*Feminism and Materialism* Routledge & Kegan Paul, London, 1978

Lacey, W.K.	*The Family in Classical Greece* Cornell University Press, New York 1968
Lefkowitz, Mary	*Heroines and Hysterics* Duckworth, London, 1981
Lefkowitz, M. & Maureen Fant	*Women's Life in Greece and Rome* Duckworth, London, 1982
Licht, Hans	*Sexual Life in Ancient Greece* George Routledge & Sons, London, 1935
Lloyd, Genevieve	*The Man of Reason* Methuen, London, 1984
	Masters, Slaves and Others Radical Philosophy, Vol. 34, summer, 1983
Lloyd, G.E.R.	*Hippocratic Writings* trans. J. Chadwick & W.N. Mann, Penguin Books, Middlesex, 1950
Lovejoy, Arthur O.	*The Great Chain of Being* Harvard University Press, London, 1936
Kay, Martin & Barbara Voorhies	*Female of the Species* Columbia University Press, New York, 1975
MacMillan, Carol	*Women, Reason & Nature* Basil Blackwell, Oxford, 1982
McClelland, David C.	*Power: The Inner Experience* John Wiley and Sons, New York, 1975
Mead, Margaret	*Male and Female* Victor Gollancz, London, 1949
Miller, Jean Baker	*Towards a New Psychology of Women* Pelican Books, Middlesex, 1976
Mitchell, Juliet	*Psychoanalysis and Feminism* Pelican Books, Middlesex, 1974
	Women's Estate Pelican Books, Middlesex, 1971
Mitchell, Juliet & Ann Oakley (ed)	*The Rights and Wrongs of Women* Pelican Books, Middlesex, 1976
Morrow, Glen	*Plato's Cretan City* Princeton University Press, New Jersey, 1960
Murdoch, Iris	*The Fire and the Sun: Why Plato Banished the Artists* Oxford University Press, Oxford, 1977
Nettleship, Richard	*An Examination of Plato's Doctrines* The Humanities Press, New York, 1962
Nye, Andrea	*Feminist Theory and the Philosophies of Man* Croom Helm, Kent, 1988

Oakley, Ann	*Sex, Gender and Society* Temple Smith, London, 1972
Oates, Whitney J. & Eugene O'Neill Jnr	*The Complete Greek Drama* Random House (14th printing), New York, 1938
O'Brien, Mary	*The Politics of Reproduction* Routledge & Kegan Paul, London, 1981
O'Faolain, Julia & Lauro Martines	*Not in God's Image* Temple Smith, London, 1973
Okin, Susan Moller	*Women in Western Political Thought* Virago, London, 1980
Orbach, Susie & Luise Eichenbaum	*What do Women Want?* Michael Joseph, London, 1983
Persall, Marilyn	*Women and Values* Wadsworth Publishing, California, 1986
Peradotto, John & J.P. Sullivan (ed)	*Women in the Ancient World* (The Arethusa Papers), State Univesity of New York Press, Albany, 1984
Pierce, Christine	*Equality: Republic V* The Monist: Vol. 57, no. 1, January, 1973
Plato	*The Collected Dialogues of Plato* Pantheon Books, New York, 1961
	Early Socratic Dialogues Penguin Classics, Middlesex, 1987
	The Last Days of Socrates (*The Euthyphro, The Apology, Crito & Phaedo*) Penguin Classics, Middlesex, 1975
	Phaedrus & Letters VII & VIII Penguin Classics, Middlesex, 1978
	Republic Penguin Classics, Middlesex, 1975
	Symposium Penguin Classics, Middlesex, 1979
	Protagoras & Meno Penguin Classics, Middlesex, 1979
	Menexenus Loeb Classical Library, 1930
	Laws Penguin Classics, Middlesex, 1970
	Timaeus & Critias Penguin Classics, Middlesex, 1965

Plato	*Gorgias* Penguin Classics, Middlesex, 1961
	Statesman Routledge, London, 1961
Pomeroy, Sarah B.	*Goddesses, Whores, Wives & Slaves* Schocken Books, New York, 1975
Popper, Karl	*The Open Society and Its Enemies* Routledge and Kegan Paul, London, 1965
Radcliffe-Richards, J.	*The Sceptical Feminist: A* *Philosophical Enquiry* Routledge & Kegan Paul, Boston, 1980
Radice, Betty & Robert Baldick (eds)	*Greek Political Oratory* Penguin Classics, Middlesex, 1970
Rankin, H.D.	*Plato and the Individual* Methuen, London, 1964
Redfield, James	*Nature and Culture in the Iliad* University of Chicago Press, Chicago, 1975
Rhodes, P.J.	*The Greek City States* Croom Helm, Kent, 1986
Rich, Adrienne	*Of Woman Born* Virago, London, 1977
Rosenthal, Abigail	*Feminism without Contradictions* The Monist, Vol. 57 no. 1, 1973
Rouse, W.H.D.	*The Great Dialogues of Plato* Plume, London, 1970
Rowbotham, Sheila	*Woman's Consciousness, Man's World* Pelican Books, Middlesex, 1973
Russell, Bertrand	*History of Western Philosophy* George Allen & Unwin, London, 1946
	The Problems of Philosophy Oxford University Press, Oxford, 1912
Saxonhouse, Arlene	*Eros and the Female in Greek* *Political Thought* Political Theory, 12, February, 1984
Saxonhouse, Arlene	*Family, Polity & Unity* Polity 15, Winter, 1982
	The Philosopher and the Female *in the Political Thought of Plato* Political Theory, 4, 1976
	Women in the History of Political *Thought* Praeger Publishers, New York, 1985
Sayers, Janet	*Sexual Contradictions* Tavistock, London, 1986

184 Bibliography

Schaps, David M. *Economic Rights of Women in Ancient Greece* Edinburgh University Press, Edinburgh, 1979

Sealey, Raphael *Women and Law in Classical Greece* University of Carolina Press, Chapel Hill and London, 1990

Seltman, Charles *Women in Antiquity* Pan Books, London, 1956

Shaw, Michael *The Female Intruder: Women in Fifth Century Drama* Classical Philology 70, October, 1975

Slater, Philip *The Glory of Hera* Beacon Press, Boston, 1971

Spender, Dale (ed) *Feminist Theorists* Women's Press, London, 1983

Stiehm, Judith (ed) *Women's Views of the Political World of Men* Transnational Publishers, New York, 1984

Strauss, Leo *The City and Man* Rand McNally, Chicago, 1964

Taylor, A.E. *Plato: The Man and his Work* Methuen, London, 1978

Thompson, Janna *Women and the High Priests of Reason* Radical Philosophy, Vol. 34, 1983

Vlastos, Gregory *Exegesis and Argument* Studies in Greek Philosophy presented to Vlastos, Van Gorum, Assen, The Netherlands, 1973

The Philosophy of Socrates Anchor Books, Garden City, New York, 1971

Was Plato a Feminist? Times Literary Supplement, London, March, 1989

Ward, Julie K. *Feminism and Ancient Philosophy* Routledge, New York/London, 1996

Webster, T.B.L. *Life in Classical Athens* B.T. Batsford, London, 1969

Whitbeck, Caroline *Theories of Sex Difference* Philosophical Forum, Vol. 5, no. 1–2, Boston, 1973–4

White, Nicholas P. *A Companion to Plato's Republic* Basil Blackwell, Oxford, 1980

Wilbur, J.B. & *The Worlds of Plato and Aristotle*

H.J. Allen	Prometheus Books, New York, 1979
Winkler, John J.	*The Constraints of Desire*
	Routledge, London, 1990
Wolff, Robert P.	*There's Nobody Here But Us Persons*
	Philosophical Forum, Vol. 5, no. 1–2,
	1973–4
Wollstonecraft, Mary	*Vindication of the Rights of*
	Women
	Penguin Classics, Middlesex, 1975
Xenophon	*Memorabilia, Oeconomicus, Symposium*
	Apology
	trans. E.C. Marchant & O.J. Todd,
	Loeb Classical Library, 1923

Index